Jay and Tracy were deep in thought and didn't bother with conversation until he pulled into the parking area before the lake that ringed Moonglow. A full moon sifted silver down through the night, adding a mystic glow to the setting.

"This is still the most romantic spot in the world," Tracy sighed, as the soft summer wind slipped over the oaks and rippled the black velvet lake.

"Yeah, it's nice here." Jay looked from the lake back to Tracy's face profiled in the moonlight.

But you're leaving soon. I think I'd better put up my defenses."

"Come on," Tracy teased. "A cool, calm detective like you keeps up his defenses."

"Once, maybe. But not anymore." The expression in his eyes was totally serious.

She decided it was time for her to be honest, as well. "I like you too, Jay. A lot. Too much. Maybe I'm the one who should leave before it's too late."

He reached out, gently pulling her against his chest. "It's already too late."

His head dipped to kiss her lips, and as they sat like stargazing teenagers, Tracy knew she had never felt like this before. Never.

Palisades.
Pure Romance.

FICTION THAT FEATURES CREDIBLE CHARACTERS AND
ENTERTAINING PLOT LINES, WHILE CONTINUING TO UPHOLD
STRONG CHRISTIAN VALUES. FROM HIGH ADVENTURE
TO TENDER STORIES OF THE HEART, EACH PALISADES
ROMANCE IS AN UNDILUTED STORY OF LOVE,
FROM BEGINNING TO END!

A PALISADES CONTEMPORARY
ROMANCE

MOONGLOW

Peggy Darty

PALISADES

This is a work of fiction. The characters, incidents, and dialogues are products of the author's imagination and are not to be construed as real. Any resemblance to actual events or persons, living or dead, is entirely coincidental.

MOONGLOW
published by Palisades
a part of the Questar publishing family

© 1997 by Peggy Darty
International Standard Book Number: 1-57673-112-X

Cover illustration by C. Michael Dudash
Cover designed by Brenda McGee

Printed in the United States of America

For information:
QUESTAR PUBLISHERS, INC.
POST OFFICE BOX 1720
SISTERS, OREGON 97759

Library of Congress Cataloging-in-Publication Data
Darty, Peggy.
    Moonglow/Peggy Darty.
        p.cm.   ISBN 1-57673-112-X (alk. paper)   I. Title.
PS3554.A79M66   1997   97-12382
813'.54--DC21   CIP

97 98 99 00 01 02 03 — 10 9 8 7 6 5 4 3 2 1

With love and thanks to Dana,
my niece and friend,
whose help with Moonglow was invaluable.

Show me the way I should go,
for to you I lift up my soul.

Prologue

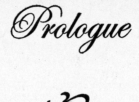

Atlanta, Georgia

Jackie DeRidder hung up the phone and smiled to herself. The exterior of Green Hills Country Club blurred slightly as she drove away, but she laughed to herself. *Maybe I had too many martinis*, she thought. She laughed again. *No, I'm simply feeling good.* Wasn't that what wealth and her new lifestyle were all about? She'd always had the looks. Now she had the money. *Jackie, girl, you've finally made it. And now you've figured out a way to get what you really want.* She smiled to herself. Yes, it was going to be a good day, after all.

Lake Lanier, Georgia

Jay Calloway lazily held his fishing rod as his boat glided along a remote shore of Lake Lanier. Coming here was one of the few things that truly relieved him of the stresses of his job as an investigator, and as he inhaled a deep breath of the fresh, moist air, he decided that he was long overdue for this. Last week he and his partner had cracked an important burglary, and the chase and arrest had been harrowing. But he could forget about that now. The criminals were behind bars and—

Just then he hooked into a huge fish—a bass. He started to play him, feeling his adrenaline soaring. As the fish flashed to the top of the water, Jay caught his breath. This was definitely a big one. At that precise moment, his pager sounded. Jay gritted his teeth, fighting the temptation to throw the pager into the deep water. Instead, he reeled in the big bass. He didn't have his scales with him, but he judged it to be almost eight pounds, bigger than the one he and Bill had caught in the tournament last spring. Grinning from ear to ear, he released the fish and watched him swim away.

"So long, Partner," he said. This was the part of fishing that brought a true reward.

Remembering his pager, he heaved a weary sigh. He checked the number, then picked up his cellular phone and dialed headquarters.

His jaw dropped at the news being delivered on the other end, and he turned his eyes far out into the distant reaches of Lake Lanier. So Jackie DeRidder was missing? He closed his eyes, picturing the look on her face—smiles and dimples— when he had last seen her. This was not going to be easy.

Los Angeles, California

Tracy Kosell paced the tile floor of her boss's office, running a nervous hand through her blonde-brown hair as she listened to Sam ramble.

Tall, thin, with a receding hairline, Sam's face rarely reflected his feelings, and now he was quite matter-of-fact as he spoke.

"Tracy, you know the deal. The reporters with seniority get to cover the Olympics."

Tracy stopped pacing and wondered if he had heard a word she had said. "Sam, we're not talking about the sports events; we're talking about the missing wife of one of the Olympics' top benefactors. We're talking about a woman I know, one I went to school with. I promise you a great story. Come on, what do you say?"

He threw his hands in the air, signaling defeat, and Tracy couldn't stop the grin of triumph slipping over her face. "You won't regret it, Sam."

She raced back to her desk, lifted the phone, and began to dial her dad's number back in Moonglow. "Hello, Dad. It's Tracy. Fine. I'm fine, really. Dad, I'll be coming home to cover the Jackie DeRidder story. Yeah, me too. I'll see you soon."

She hung up the receiver and stared over the heads of the busy newsroom. For a moment she closed her eyes, scarcely believing that at last she was going back to Georgia. If she and God had been on speaking terms, she'd have asked him for help with this project. As it was, she would face going home the way she'd faced so many things lately. Alone.

One

"Hi, Dad!"

Tracy Kosell stood on the front porch of the white frame house and stared through the screen at the father she hadn't seen for six months. Not since the funeral.

"Tracy!" Richard Kosell opened the door and extended his arms. As Tracy stepped into his embrace, she could feel the awkwardness of it, but she tried to remember a thousand other bear hugs when there hadn't been an undertow of tension between them.

She could smell the faint whiff of a pleasant aftershave as her arms slid around his strong back. Her fingers pressed into the soft flesh, feeling the extra weight. No one was monitoring his diet now, and he was probably frying chicken every other day.

"How was the flight from L.A.?" he asked, frowning. "I can tell you I've been plenty worried, what with the recent plane tragedies."

"I know. My flight was okay, but I was shaky too," she admitted, looking up into the round face, the hazel eyes that had lost some of their twinkle. "Anyway, I'm here safe and sound. The worst part of the trip was getting from the airport to the freeway."

"I can imagine. Come on in," he said, waving an arm.

Richard Kosell was five feet eleven inches, with medium brown hair that was thinning on top, thick brows over hazel eyes, broad cheeks, and an agreeable smile. He wore casual gray slacks and a button-down shirt with pale blue pinstripes, open at the collar.

"You've lost weight," he said matter-of-factly, as his eyes ran down her petite frame.

"And you've gained," she retorted, then quickly grinned. This time they were going to get along, she warned herself.

"Just a few pounds." He looked sheepish, as his eyes swept down his thick middle. Then he turned back to his daughter, looked her over, and smiled. "You look good, Tracy."

"Thanks," she said quietly. She was five feet three inches tall, with a trim figure that she credited to a busy schedule. She turned her eyes toward the living room, looking around.

"Well, you've kept everything nice," she said, already feeling the tightness clutch at her throat as her eyes scanned the cozy room.

The house was a simple ranch style, with three bedrooms and a bath. A foyer led into a living room on one side, a dining room on the other. Behind these, a den and kitchen were combined, separated by an eating bar. The foyer curved to the right, leading to two bedrooms with a connecting bath on one side and a master bedroom and bath on the other. On the back of the house, her dad had built a small deck, and Mom had made the cushions for lawn furniture. Throughout the house, the furniture was Early American, mostly maple, except for a marble-topped stand and a mahogany secretary, the latter inherited from her great-grandmother's small estate.

Nothing was changed, but then why would it be? In fact, it

all looked so natural that she expected to smell bread baking and see her mother suddenly appear in the arched doorway leading to the kitchen. Her face would be slightly flushed from the heat of the oven, and the humidity would have curled the waves about her pretty oval face. She would brush it back from large brown eyes—eyes that always glowed with love. That memory brought a rush of emotion and Tracy swallowed hard.

"So, you're here to cover the Jackie DeRidder story," her father said hurriedly, as though reading her thoughts and sensing a need to change the subject.

"That's right. I can't wait to ask what you know about it. But first, I should get my things out of the car."

"Let me help you," he offered. "Then we can sit down with some lemonade. I've just made a fresh batch."

"Good idea." Tracy tucked a strand of hair behind her ear. Her sister, Beth, had the curls; Tracy had the waves, styled in a short bob that bounced just above her shoulders. Half bangs slanted across her forehead. "Can't wait to taste it," she said, following him down the hall.

As she passed the gold-framed mirror over her great-grandmother's table, Tracy recognized the look of her father's family stamped across her face. He was still a handsome man, with nice features, but she was thankful that her features were smaller, softer. A square jawbone was balanced by a pair of full red lips, small nose and a high forehead. Huge hazel eyes twinkled beneath brows like her father's, which kept her busy tweezing their thickness into a smooth arch. She had her mother's button nose, which softened "that determined look" her mother often described.

As she glanced back at her father, he was staring into her face now, and for a moment, Tracy couldn't help wondering what he was seeing there.

"Well, let's get your bags," he said, his tone softened by

whatever thought had just drifted through his mind. Did he see a resemblance to her mother for once? She doubted it. He would have looked at sweet Mary Elisabeth to see her mother, and he did. Often.

"How's Beth and the family?" Tracy asked, hearing the strident note slip into her tone. It was always the same. No matter how much she tried to appreciate her older sister, that slight twinge of guilt—yes, even jealousy—always nudged at her.

"They're doing well. She's anxious to see you."

Tracy took a deep breath. *I'll bet. She can't wait to remind me of all the things I didn't say and do.*

You abandoned them when they needed you most! The words screamed through her mind, although Beth wasn't a screamer. She could deliver a simple sentence in a way that managed to irritate Tracy nonetheless.

"Want to give me the car keys and let me get your bags?" Her father had turned back at the door. He seemed to notice that she had drifted off into space again.

"No, I'll come along." She forced a smile, even though it felt unnatural to her now. "We won't bring everything into the house. Just the overnighter. I'll be staying in Atlanta."

He paused on the porch step, beside the clay pot that held colorful splotches of red, purple, and pink. Tracy stared at the petunias, thinking of her mother again.

"I guess if you're going to cover a story taking place in Atlanta, you need to be in Atlanta," Richard Kosell conceded. "And it isn't practical to think of your driving an hour and a half from here into the city. Still…"

Tracy took a deep breath, feeling a more professional attitude take hold at the mention of her work. It was like slipping into a coat on a cold evening. Work was comforting, all encompassing, a shield against the forces of emotion.

"I'll try to spend the weekends here," she said, catching up

18

with him on the porch steps. "After all, I need to relax a bit, too."

They were walking together down the concrete sidewalk that centered two perfect patches of green yard. Her father still kept the yard in mint condition, she noticed.

"Well, you can count on Moonglow for relaxation," he responded. "The town is growing a bit, with the overflow of tourist traffic veering off the main highway to investigate us. Still, the place is an escape from traffic and crime."

Tracy took a deep breath, absorbing the pine scent and feeling the promise of mountain air. Turning her eyes north, she could see the Blue Ridge Mountains far in the distance. She recalled the hiking trails and the cool splash of the river from rafting trips in the summer.

Her father turned at the foot of the walk, frowning back at her. "How do you stand it out there?"

"In L.A., you mean? It's exciting, Dad. Lots of places to go, neat restaurants, fun people."

He merely shrugged. Tracy knew he couldn't relate to what she was saying.

"And I enjoy my work," she flung at his back as he trudged toward the car. His shoulders had rounded just a bit the past year, she noticed, and he moved more slowly. He actually seemed older than his fifty-eight years.

They had reached the white Maxima, parked beside his sturdy blue Buick. "Nice rental car," he said.

"I tried to select something that would get good gas mileage," she answered.

This time his eyes twinkled as he grinned at her. "Good girl."

She turned and glanced around the yard. Her eyes paused on the gazebo they had built as a family building project one summer. Upon completion of it, they had made homemade ice cream and invited friends over. Her mother had made her special caramel cake.

"Incidentally, that newscast comes on at five," her father was saying. "You'll want to see it. I hear Jay Calloway is one of the lead investigators."

"Jay?" Tracy stopped walking, puzzled.

"That's right. And being from Moonglow didn't give him the edge, either. From all indications, he's a first-class detective."

"Hmmm." Tracy bit her lip, seeing in her mind's eye the tall, lanky guy at her study-hall table. He was three years older than she, and he used to be a bit shy, but everyone had liked him.

"Isn't that a coincidence?" she asked, hooking her makeup bag over her shoulder.

"A coincidence?" Her dad was pulling out her suitcase.

"Jay and I are both from Moonglow, same place as Jackie, and now we're both working on her disappearance. From different angles, of course."

"I see what you mean," he said, slamming the trunk and removing the keys from the lock.

Tracy followed her dad back up the front steps and entered the house again. Her dad led the way down the hall, past Beth's room. It looked the same as always: a proper white lace canopy over a neat bed with white lace pillows. All so like Beth. Tracy winced and pushed on, following her father into the colorful pastel room that was hers. Now this was more like it.

She took a deep breath as her eyes moved over her old room. She had insisted on a pale yellow room so that she could feel that every day was sunny when she awoke. Her bedspread was a bright floral print, and on the walls she had tacked lots of memorabilia from school days. A picture of the Yellow Jacket cheerleaders, forming the pyramid. She was in the second row, a lopsided grin on her face, her short hair dipping over her forehead. On her dresser was a framed newspaper clipping from college days featuring some of the star reporters from her journalism class. She looked more sophisticated in this photo, and yet she still had that impishness about her. *Guess I'll never change,* she thought as she studied the photos.

In the center of her bed, wearing a baseball cap, was Ernie, her overstuffed teddy bear. It had taken every ounce of willpower not to pack him up when she left for college.

Her dad was placing her overnight bag beside the louvered closet doors. "Thanks, Dad."

"As soon as you get settled in, come on back to the den. The news will be on in about five minutes."

"I'll be there." She laid her purse across the bed and reached forward, lifting Ernie to give him a squeeze. He was as soft and cuddly as ever, and she couldn't wait to cuddle up to him tonight as she lay in bed, recalling her high school days.

Her eyes drifted to the open door as she heard her father's steps retreating to the den.

She walked over, crossed the hall, and stood staring into her parents' room. Her mother's stamp was everywhere: the needlepoint pillows, the soft white afghan spread over the cherry fourposter. On the dresser, she saw mostly her father's things, except for an eight-by-ten of her parents, taken for the church directory the year before her mother died.

Tracy took a deep breath and clutched the door frame as pain swept her like a tidal wave. Her dad had always told her that God was a loving Father, intimately concerned with every aspect of life. But if that were so, how could a loving Father rip her mother, her anchor, away so callously?

And how could a loving daughter turn away from her mother when she needed her most? her heart accused in response.

I didn't turn away! she argued. *It wasn't like that at all. I just...I just couldn't face it.*

Maybe it isn't like you think it is with God, either.

21

One of her dad's favorite Scriptures floated into her mind. "I will never leave you nor forsake you." She bit her lip, struggling with tears. She wanted to believe, to trust again. But there was so much holding her back.

She turned from the room and took a deep breath, trying to cast her troubled thoughts aside, at least for a while. Squaring her shoulders, she marched resolutely to the den, pushing her mind toward the newscast, toward Jackie DeRidder and her mysterious disappearance or kidnapping or whatever had happened to her.

As she reached the den, she saw the pitcher of lemonade on the eating bar, along with two large glasses. "Ah, my favorite treat," she said, hurriedly crossing the beige carpet to pour lemonade. Sipping the drink, she nestled into the overstuffed sofa. It was a room of comfort and home, a place to unwind and relax. She glanced at the coffee table, holding a stack of newspapers and magazines, with the Bible and a concordance nearby. An assortment of her dad's keys rested in a ceramic bowl; beneath the coffee table she spotted his house shoes. Obviously, he spent most of his time here when at home.

The anchor on the evening newscast was speaking as a picture of Jackie flashed over the screen. Tracy stared at her, hardly recognizing the girl she remembered from high school. A gorgeous woman smiled from a photograph. Blonde hair framed an oval face, with just the right touch of foundation, eyeliner, and blush to show off nice features, large blue eyes, and a winning smile over straight white teeth.

"Jacqueline DeRidder was last seen leaving Green Hills Country Club just after twelve on Friday," the news anchor was saying. "She has not been seen or heard from since, and there is now a reward for any information leading to her whereabouts. She was last seen driving her black '96 Mercedes, license number JLD 395."

Her picture disappeared from the screen, and the camera flashed to the police station in downtown Atlanta. A cameraman and reporter had centered on Jay Calloway.

"Mr. Calloway, any news on Mrs. DeRidder?"

The camera zeroed in on his face, and Tracy leaned forward, hands on her knees, studying the man who had been her school chum. Jay had turned into a handsome man. The slim, boyish face she remembered had now matured into one with wide green eyes, pronounced cheekbones, and an angular jawline. His dark brown hair was modestly cut and probably the envy of every woman he knew. In a navy suit with white shirt and wine-colored tie, he was the kind of man any woman would notice.

"We're following all leads," Jay replied smoothly, "and are optimistic about locating Mrs. DeRidder soon. Now, if you'll excuse me." With that he tactfully sidestepped the reporter, who then turned back to face the camera.

"That was Jay Calloway, one of the investigators in the disappearance of Jackie DeRidder. Again, if anyone has any information of her whereabouts..." The reporter droned on, repeating the description of the car and the license number as Tracy turned to her father.

"Dad, what do you think happened to Jackie? Do you think a kidnapper is just biding his time on a ransom call?"

"Would seem that way," Richard replied, getting up from the recliner. "It would be hard for a blonde woman in a black Mercedes to vanish into thin air." He glanced at his watch, then back at her.

Tracy could see the question forming in his mind. She held her breath, waiting for him to ask.

"Will you be joining us this evening?"

Tracy swallowed. "Actually, Dad, I'm really beat. I was on

standby at the airport for hours. I didn't even know I was coming until yesterday when Jackie's disappearance hit the wires. I had to pack in a hurry and—"

He threw up his hand, halting her nervous flow. "I understand. There's a pot roast and vegetables on top of the stove. Betty Jo and Bill brought over some extras, knowing you were coming home."

"That was sweet." Tracy's eyes softened, remembering the music director at church, who was always so considerate of everyone's needs.

"Well, I had better freshen up," he said, turning toward the hall.

She bit her lip, at a loss for words. What could she say? Her father would preach yet another sermon without seeing her face in the third row.

Two

J ay Calloway had already been assailed by one news team; now another lurked for him in the parking lot. He mentally took stock of his situation, calling forth every ounce of patience, but his patience was running thin. He still hadn't gotten his life back in order since last Friday, when the phone call had come at Lake Lanier. Nothing had settled into place since.

He checked the condition of his suit and decided he would pass inspection. The suit had gone with him through a meeting with the mayor, a representative from the FBI, and one taped TV interview.

He stretched his neck against the tight collar of his white shirt while his hand absently smoothed his tie. Although it was early evening, the humidity was still heavy; he could feel his shirt sticking to his shoulder blades beneath his lightweight jacket. He took a deep breath of the muggy Atlanta air, inhaling the fumes of traffic and hot asphalt, then winced. He longed to be holed up at Lake Lanier, relaxing. Or even back in Moonglow, breathing in the fresh air that floated down from the Blue Ridge Mountains. He had chosen this line of work, however, and even though the job was challenging, he had to admit to himself that it was one he loved.

He forced himself to slow his usual long stride to accommodate the attractive blonde woman making a dash in his direction—Suzy Greenwood from Channel 6. Behind her, a big man hoisted a television camera on his broad shoulder and struggled to keep up. The eye of the camera was aimed directly at Jay's face.

"Could we get a statement from you, Mr. Calloway?" Ms. Greenwood flashed her famous smile.

He nodded. "As long as we can be brief. I'm late for an appointment." He glanced at his watch. He was being truthful. He hadn't eaten since breakfast, and his favorite Italian chef was always eager to have him drop in. Furthermore, this was his night to take T. J. to the circus near his home in Smyrna. Jay was a member of Big Brothers, and T. J. came from a home where his single mom had five other children to care for on a limited income. T. J. was five years old and had become very special to Jay.

The camera light was on now, and Suzy summarized what was known about Jackie DeRidder's disappearance. Then she introduced Jay to the thousands and thousands of news seekers who would stare at him through their television screen. People who would evaluate not only what he said but the way he said it. While Suzy thrust the microphone in Jay's face, the big cameraman zeroed in.

"And can you give us the latest news on the disappearance of Mrs. DeRidder, Mr. Calloway?"

"We're following all leads," he replied carefully, hoping he sounded more polite than he felt. "And we're optimistic about locating Mrs. DeRidder soon." He smiled into the camera, then back at Suzy. "Now if you'll excuse me."

"Thank you." She was all white teeth and dimples as she faced the camera.

"That was Jay Calloway…" he could hear her explaining his

part in the investigation as he swiftly made his exit.

Once he reached the parking lot, he spotted Bill, his partner, waiting for him beside their unmarked car. Bill was forty-five, divorced, and remarried to his job. He lived and breathed police work. Shorter than Jay by at least five inches, Bill had an odd way of looking at him. He tilted his head to the right and leveled a sideways glance toward Jay. Jay thought it had something to do with Bill's not wanting to look directly up at him and thus acknowledge the contrast in stature.

"Glad the media likes your looks better than mine," Bill chuckled.

Jay shook his head, feeling completely drained after the past three days of following every lead, dealing with the media, and trying to learn everything about the DeRidder lifestyle without stepping on Martin DeRidder's sensitive toes. "Let's get out of here."

"What's the hurry?" Bill glanced over his shoulder at Suzy Greenwood, who was still talking into the camera. "I thought you liked blondes."

"Come on, Bill." He yanked open the car door. "Give me a break!"

Later, with T. J. chattering away in the passenger's seat, Jay found an empty space in the parking lot and parked the car, then glanced across at his little friend. T. J. was small for his age, with curly black hair and dark skin. His hair shot up in a cowlick directly on his crown. No matter how many times his hair was smoothed down, several little hairs popped back up, giving him an almost comical appearance. He had big, dark eyes, a crooked grin, and was wearing a clean, though faded, T-shirt, well-worn jeans, and the new tennis shoes Jay had bought him for his birthday.

"Hey, T. J. Ready to go see the lions and tigers?"

"I can't wait, can you, Jay?"

"Nope. Let me come around and get you out though. I can't risk you darting out in traffic again." That had happened once before when he was taking T. J. to a Braves game, and the incident had scared the wits out of Jay. T. J. was lightning fast, and in his eagerness to get to the stadium, he had darted in front of a car. Jay had tackled him, and they had both rolled out of the path of the car, but it was a lesson Jay had never forgotten.

"Look, Jay, a TV camera!" T. J. pointed, squirming eagerly in the car seat. His face was pressed directly against the car window.

"Sure is." Everywhere Jay went he seemed to be running into a television camera, but he was relieved to see that this one appeared to be a simple interview of children attending the circus. A crowd had gathered around the young man with the microphone that bore the insignia of the station.

"Let's see what's going on," Jay said, hopping out of the car and coming around to get T. J. Taking a firm grip on the little hand, Jay steered him toward the crowd. Children were stumbling over cables and had to be herded back into a neat line.

"Everyone ready?" the television host was asking the group of wide-eyed children. "Don't be afraid of the camera or the microphone. All you have to do is tell me what you like most about the circus. Think you can handle that?"

A chorus of enthusiastic responses filled the air as the boys and girls nudged each other, then stood impatiently waiting. The camera lit up as the television personality spoke, his rich, deep voice ringing out across the crowd. "Come to the circus! Join the razzle-dazzle in the big arena where a sell-out crowd is gathering. The circus came to Smyrna today, and the entire town seems to have captured the excitement. Why do people come to the circus?" his voice rose questioningly, his dark head inclined in a gesture of curiosity. "We decided to ask the real experts."

He leaned down, extending the microphone to a small, blonde boy whose blue eyes had widened to enormous proportions. "I came to see Dumbo the elephant," he volunteered.

"I came to see the clowns," a little girl giggled as the man moved the microphone along the group.

Jay nudged T. J. "Want to be on television?"

T. J.'s dark eyes were huge in his thin face. "Yeah, then I can tell everybody at school!"

Jay guided him gently toward the group, giving him a slight nudge toward the microphone.

T. J. took the initiative. "I like to see the pretty girls up on the high wire!"

The commentator laughed along with the other children and turned back to the camera.

"Whatever the reason, there's nothing quite like a circus to make all of us feel young at heart."

Jay chuckled to himself, grabbing T. J.'s hand again and hustling him on toward the ticket booth. "You're famous now," he said to T. J., whose little chest had thrust forward importantly.

Later, on the way home from the circus, T. J. talked incessantly about the wonders he had seen—fourteen cages of tigers, prowling on velvet paws; great white stallions, muscles of steel rippling beneath satin coats; high-wire artists performing their death-defying stunts on wire suspended in space.

"Did you have a good time, Jay?" T. J. shouted. There was no point in trying to shush him down. He was worked up to a fever pitch. Jay felt sorry for his mother after he got home. He should offer to take him to an ice-cream parlor, but he could scarcely keep his eyes open now. The DeRidder case had taken its toll, and there was always the possibility that he could get paged at any moment to chase down a potential suspect.

T. J. was staring at him, his little head tilted, as though he expected an answer. Remembering the question, Jay grinned at him. "Yeah, T. J., I had a great time." Jay answered.

"Can we go to another circus?" T. J. wanted to know.

"When another one comes," Jay agreed. It was good to be with T. J., sharing his simple boyish pleasures while forgetting all the hassles of his job as a detective. He turned into the shabby apartment complex where T. J. lived. This was a neighborhood of gangs and drugs, where muggings happened in open daylight. Jay glanced at the excited boy beside him. *At least one kid might be diverted from going in the wrong direction,* Jay thought. Being a Big Brother seemed like a small thing for him to do, even though tonight every bone in his body ached. And he couldn't leave his work behind when he went home at night. Even at the circus as he sat beside T. J., trying to muster up some enthusiasm about the acts going on, his mind kept going back to Jackie DeRidder. In fact, no matter where he went or what he did, he couldn't seem to stop thinking of her.

Three

A filet for breakfast, Dad?" Tracy stared at the platter holding two steaks. A bagel and orange juice were her usual fare, with the bagel being devoured on the run. She blinked sleepily as her father brandished a serving fork into his masterpiece and laid it gently across her plate.

"Nothing but the best for my daughter."

Was there something suspicious about his tone? Tracy wondered. Was he being sarcastic?

Dropping her eyes to the napkin she was unfolding in her lap, she mentally scolded herself for being so cynical. When she looked at him again, there was a pleasant smile on her face. "Steak and eggs and grits," she said, shaking her head. "Honestly, I'm not used to eating like this." She looked pointedly at the way the shirt strained over his midriff, but he didn't seem to notice.

"You look like you've missed too many meals lately," he said, as his hazel eyes flicked down her white T-shirt and jeans.

Automatically, her glance followed his. "I have slim arms and legs that never seem to show the weight. It's the middle I have to watch out for."

He chuckled, taking a seat. "I'll say grace."

She bowed her head, listening to his humble prayer. Again she felt a stab of guilt for not attending his service last night.

Don't start hounding yourself again, an inner voice spoke up. *It'll be too much like the other times.* She remembered how miserable those were.

"Where will you be staying in Atlanta?" her father asked.

"I got lucky. My boss has a friend who's an Atlanta realtor. Fortunately for me, a couple had just canceled out on a rental place in Buckhead. There was a life-threatening illness in their family, and they couldn't leave London."

"Must have cost a bundle to get into Buckhead."

"It did, but my boss allowed me an expense account. It's pretty meager so I decided to dig into my savings. This is vacation and work, all in one. After living in a studio apartment for the past year, I think I've earned a little extravagance. And the location is in walking distance of the best restaurants in Buckhead. Also, it's not too far from the DeRidder house."

"Are you going to the DeRidder house?" His brows shot up in surprise.

"If I can get an interview with someone. If not, I'll just go by and check it out several times, try to get a feel for Jackie's lifestyle. If that's possible," she added, shaking her head. "Boy, Jackie really married into the money, Dad."

He said nothing for a moment as he handed her a bowl of grits. Then, after a pause, he looked at her with an expression she understood. A challenge. "You reckon it made her happy?"

Tracy suppressed a sigh. She should have known her father would have to point out the moral side of things. She reached for the grits, ladled out a generous serving, then returned to the eggs.

"I wouldn't know," she said tightly, averting her eyes to the table. While her father had not used a tablecloth or the linen napkins, as her mother would have done, he had served break-fast on her mother's everyday china rather than the plastic standbys. "Well," she tried again, "no food in Atlanta will compare to yours. I had forgotten what a good cook you are."

"I enjoy cooking, always have."

Tracy's thoughts drifted back to her mother's Sunday dinners, the chicken casseroles, her special fruit salads, the made-from-scratch cakes. Then she became conscious of the silence. She suspected the same thoughts must be occupying her father's mind as well. *He must get lonely,* she thought miserably, but she didn't want to broach the subject. Not yet.

"You be careful driving around in all that traffic," he spoke up suddenly, his words coming in a rush. "I read there may be a million people in Atlanta for the Olympics. Talk about a traffic jam...." He shook his head.

"I'll be taking good ol' MARTA into the city. Don't you want me to see if I can get you a ticket for one of the events, Dad?" She would welcome a chance to do something for him.

He shook his head, taking a hearty bite of steak. "I've been keeping up by television. About the only thing I'd like a seat for is one of those peach cobblers at Aunt Pittypat's Porch."

At the mention of one of Atlanta's most popular restaurants, Tracy's thoughts turned to Atlanta and the story she had come to write.

"Which reminds me," she sighed, "I'd better get going."

He nodded. "When can you come back?"

There was a note of tension in his voice; she could hear it, feel it. No matter how hard they both tried—and she knew that he was trying—there was still this unresolved pain between them. And neither seemed capable of doing anything about it.

"Dad, I'll try to come back this weekend," she said. She wanted to make things right—she just didn't seem to know how.

"This is a dream come true," Tracy said as she passed through the iron gates to the carriage house in Buckhead. Beyond the brick walls surrounding the courtyard she could hear the hum of traffic along Peachtree and West Paces Ferry. But within these walls she seemed to have stepped into a magical garden. She stopped at the door, depositing her bags on the step while she fished into her handbag for the keys. Her eyes explored the brick exterior, up past the flower boxes bursting with red geraniums, and on to the gabled windows. This was going to be fun.

Armed with luggage, she stepped lightly over the gleaming hardwood floor. She set down her things and looked around sea-green walls to the comfortable furniture. The furnishings were a mix of old and new, an antique here and there interspersed with thick, solid comfort. An overstuffed sofa and chair, upholstered in red, cream, and yellow, set up a relaxed, cheerful atmosphere. The antique bookcase held collectibles, classic novels, and antique picture frames.

"Ah, welcome home," she said, closing the door behind her.

On the wall beside the door, a triple window was framed by draperies the color of rich cream. Through the window, she had a view of the courtyard, which held plants, blooming flowers, and a wrought-iron table and chairs with bright cushions. It looked like the perfect place for having morning coffee and reading the paper. Quite an improvement over the view from her window in L.A., which was the freeway!

She peered into the kitchen, small yet convenient and homey, and there was a cozy little bath adjoining the living room. Reclaiming her load, she climbed the steps to the upper story.

Upstairs, a hall separated two bedrooms and a bath. Peering

into the smaller one, she saw that it was designed as an office/workout room with treadmill and stereo system. A futon sat against the wall. In the cozy bath, a pedestal sink and a porcelain, claw-footed tub caught her eye.

She turned into the larger bedroom, looking over the soft yellow walls and breathing a sigh of contentment. The windows were draped with lace sheers and topped with balloon valances of sea green. It was a soothing, restful room. Beside the front window a loveseat and chair provided a perfect place to read or just relax.

Her eyes moved on to the elegant four-poster covered with a Battenburg-lace comforter, green and yellow pillows. Suddenly thoughts of her mother's room in Moonglow slipped into her mind, and tears swam in her eyes. This was getting hard. It was far easier to keep the memories at bay when she was on the West Coast.

There was more than enough room in the closet for her clothes, considering her brief stay, and as she started to unpack, she took a deep, long breath. It seemed odd for her to be so comfortable covering a story while Jackie DeRidder, her subject, was probably suffering at someone's hands.

Her thoughts circled back to Jay, and her eyes strayed to the bedside phone. On a whim, she decided to phone him.

Taking a seat in the chair beside the telephone, she located a phone directory in the drawer of the nightstand. Feeling the weight in her hand, she stared at the phone directory. Atlanta was growing!

Anxiously, she began to flip through the pages of the directory. *He's probably unlisted*, she thought, running her finger down the columns of Cs. To her surprise, she saw his name. She recognized the initials—J. W.—James Walter, but everyone called him Jay, she remembered, smiling. He had a brother, Michael, two years older. She stared at the number and the name, somewhat amazed that she would still remember all of that after all these years.

Repeating the numbers aloud, she lifted the phone and began to dial. Glancing at her watch, she saw that it was only three in the afternoon. He was probably not at home.

A pleasant voice came on the answering machine: "Sorry I missed you.... Leave a message." She cleared her throat, waiting for the beep.

"Hi, Jay, this is Tracy Kosell. Remember me? I'm here from L.A. doing a story on Jackie DeRidder. I was wondering if we could meet." She glanced at the phone, reading the number lettered on the tiny white square. She gave him the number and said good-bye.

With that done, she returned to her unpacking, wondering how long it would be until she heard from him.

To her surprise, the phone rang within the hour. She was puttering around the kitchen, making tea and contemplating whom to call first to establish contact for her story.

When she answered the phone, a smooth, deep voice spoke up. "This is Jay Calloway returning a call to Tracy Kosell."

"Hi, Jay! It's me. How've you been?"

"Fine, and you?"

"Very well. You got my message, so you know why I called."

"Yes, where are you?"

"I'm staying in Buckhead, just off Peachtree and West Paces Ferry." She gave him the house number.

"I live on Peachtree-Dunwoody," he answered pleasantly. "I'm not far from you. Do you have dinner plans?"

She twirled the phone cord around her finger, excited at the prospect of seeing him so soon.

"Why, no. I just got here."

"Good," Jay responded. "I need to talk with someone at the Fish Market Restaurant near you. Does seafood appeal to you?"

"Always," she laughed. "I can meet you there."

"Sure, or I can pick you up."

She hesitated. "I'll just meet you there," she said, feeling her independent nature take over.

"Fine. Is eight okay?"

"Terrific. Thanks, Jay."

"My pleasure. I'll look forward to seeing you."

Tracy hung up the phone and shook her head. So he only lived a few blocks away. *What a coincidence*, she thought again, hurrying upstairs for a bath.

Four

The Fish Market was bustling with the evening crowd when Jay arrived. Looking around, he didn't see Tracy in the line waiting on the wide porch or in the comfortable-looking rocking chairs. But then he hadn't expected her to be thirty minutes early.

Sidestepping the crowd, he entered the front door and glanced around for Tom Hollingsworth, the assistant manager. He spotted him in conversation with the hostess. As Jay approached, he could hear bits and pieces of their conversation concerning a long table in the rear being set up for the large group assembled together just inside the door.

When Tom spotted Jay, he waved and made his way around the crowd, smiling as he did so. Tom knew how to handle his diners.

"Jay, nice to see you." He extended his hand. "You wanted to know about Trey, but he hasn't been a server here all week." He lowered his voice. "Is he in trouble?"

"No, I just wanted to talk to him."

Jay followed Tom to a private alcove and explained why he had asked to speak to Trey. Trey Gilmore had been one of the witnesses to a hit-and-run accident on Peachtree, and so Jay was checking out the young man's character references since his statement was crucial to the case.

Tom gave him a glowing report, which Jay had expected. After all, he wouldn't want an employee who wasn't considered a good citizen.

"Thanks, Tom. That's all I needed to know. Got a table?"

Tom grinned. "Always have a table for you. Are you dining alone?"

"Actually I'm meeting someone for a change." Jay glanced back over his shoulder toward the door. "I'll see if she's here."

His thoughts moved back to Tracy Kosell, the cute little gal from high school. He'd always thought she was one of the most attractive girls in school, but the fact that she was a preacher's kid had caused him to keep his distance. He wasn't sure why. Maybe she'd seemed too...good. Too perfect. Besides, he had always been the shy type unless someone made him feel especially comfortable—as Jackie had during high school days. He winced at that thought and forced his mind back to Tracy. He wondered what to expect now, as he pushed the door open and glanced around the porch.

The hostess called a name, and a young woman jumped from the rocker, joining her date. In the adjoining rocker, he spotted Tracy and did a double take. She had turned into a knockout. She had smooth skin with good bone structure and beautiful small features, except for wide hazel eyes. Her hair was the kind of blonde-brown that captured the sunlight and haloed her face. And he remembered how those hazel eyes turned on like lights when she got excited about something. He took a deep breath and slipped his hands in his pockets, hoping to appear casual.

Five

"Tracy?" A voice called from behind her.

Tracy turned and caught her breath. Jay Calloway looked even better in person than he did on television. He was no longer lanky with a shy look in those gorgeous green eyes. His six-foot frame had muscled out just right: broad shoulders slimmed to a narrow torso and long legs. He looked wonderful in khakis and a brown linen shirt.

"Hi, Jay." She smiled into his tan face.

"You look terrific," he said, glancing down her ivory silk blouse and flowing print skirt. She wore tan leather sandals and carried a matching handbag. Her only jewelry was a pair of large, silver hoop earrings, which she had purchased at an open air market down in Mexico.

"Thanks. And you look well." She smiled at him. "It's been awhile, hasn't it?"

He nodded as his eyes trailed over her face. "Yes, it has. Listen, I already have a table for us. I was inside speaking to the assistant manager when you walked up."

"The assistant manager. And did this have anything to do with the DeRidder case?" she asked teasingly.

He took her arm, steering her around the crowd. "Are you hungry?"

So mind your own business, Tracy, she thought, grinning at him. The smell of seafood greeted her, along with the marvelous aroma of fresh-baked bread. A hunger pain hit the pit of her stomach. "I'm famished," she said.

"We can select our own fish or order the catch of the day. What appeals to you?"

She looked up into his eyes. "Honestly? Southern-fried catfish. Can I get that here?"

He chuckled. "I'm sure you can."

The dining room was a wide, open room with booths and tables. Huge fish tanks featured live lobsters and trout. At the opposite end, mounds of ice with clams and oysters ready to be shucked waited for hungry diners. In spite of the din created by the open room, the dining room had an aura of coziness.

Tom led them to a table where a server rushed forward to get drink orders. Both chose iced tea.

"Catch me up on yourself," Jay said, leaning back in the chair. His green eyes darkened as he looked her over again.

"After the University of Georgia, I went to work in the newsroom of CNN. I lived in Atlanta for a year. Then I took off to L.A. to work for the West Coast office. That's where the—" she made quotation marks with her fingers—"big money was supposed to be. It was there or New York, and I wanted to see the West Coast. My second year in L.A., I got a job offer with the Associated Press, and that's where I've stayed for the past two years."

"You've been a busy girl," he said, glancing at the salads being delivered.

"Yeah, you could say that." She forked into her salad, thinking about the hectic year she had just spent.

"So what do you think of the West Coast?" Jay asked.

Tracy glanced at him. She thought it was interesting the way he studied her, exactly as she would have expected a good detective to do. There was a polite expression on his face; his questions were simple enough, and yet she'd bet those thoughtful green eyes didn't miss an expression or the slightest change in her mood or tone of voice.

She touched the napkin to her lips. "It's a different lifestyle from our laid-back south. Actually, Atlanta isn't so laid back," she said smiling, "but compared to Moonglow...."

He chuckled, a rich, deep sound that Tracy liked. There was a genuineness to his laughter that made her want to join in. "Good ol' Moonglow," he drawled.

Tracy felt a thrill race over her just listening to him speak. She had always been proud of her Southern accent, even though she had been teased about it in L.A. Now, listening to Jay, she knew she had missed that "Southern gentleman" image. He didn't bite his words the way so many guys in the West Coast newsroom did; he caressed each one, and she liked the effect. She blinked and tried to focus on what he was saying.

"I haven't been out to the coast and don't think I care to go. Atlanta is cosmopolitan enough for me. My work schedule hasn't permitted much vacation time. When I do get some time off, I'm more likely to grab a rod and reel and head for the lake. Then I'll get called back in on a case." He sighed. "I was at Lake Lanier the day Jackie DeRidder disappeared."

She took a deep breath. "Too bad you don't get more time off. Lake Lanier is nice." Then she remembered something. "Weren't you on one of our church trips to Tallulah Gorge?"

He laughed. "Didn't think you'd remember. I had just hit adolescence, and I was terrified of girls. Particularly you."

"Me?" she arched an eyebrow. "Oh, yeah, I was real intimidating with my ponytail and braces."

He winked. "I always thought you were kind of cute. Maybe

43

I should say I was scared of your father."

"Of Dad? Why, he's a big teddy bear."

He grinned and nodded agreeably. "He's a nice man. I guess I was just frightened by the prospect of dating the preacher's daughter."

She sighed and her smile faded. "You and half the other males I knew. Why was that?" She tilted her head sideways and studied him from an angle. Any way you looked at Jay, he was one fine-looking male. She couldn't believe she hadn't noticed that before. And he was a very nice person. Quite a combination. One she could truly appreciate after being on her own for several years and meeting all types. A brief memory of Howard Davis Hampton III—Howie—flashed through her mind, and she breathed a sigh of relief. Thank God that relationship was over.

"Felt I had to be the perfect guy if I was dating the preacher's daughter," Jay continued. "Although I know now that being a Christian isn't being perfect, just being forgiven. Or something like that." He took a sip of tea, looking at her over the glass.

Suddenly uncomfortable, she shifted in her chair and immediately sought a safer topic.

"So when did you decide to go into police work?"

His lips tilted in that same boyish grin that Tracy remembered and liked. It wasn't a shy grin, more a lazy one, like he was going to lean back and stretch before he made a response. Probably threw many a criminal into thinking this guy was a bit slow, but she remembered how smart he had been in school, and she knew he had a quick mind.

"You know how some kids think they want to be a fireman or a policeman?" he asked. "They get the outfits for Christmas and are still wearing them in summer. Well, that was me. I always wanted to be in law enforcement. Always. It kept my life relatively simple because there was no confusion about what I would do when I graduated from high school. I went to college, then the police academy, took some special courses, and became an investigator. Actually, I've loved every minute of my career. Until lately. With the tension in the air from plane crashes and an underlying fear floating around the Olympic Village..." His voice trailed off. Then he glanced back at her. "I can't see myself in any other line of work, though."

She nodded, watching his green eyes glow as he spoke of his life. He seemed to really care about his work.

"What about your job?" he asked. "Did you come to cover the Olympics and then get sidetracked with the DeRidder case?"

She grinned. "Actually, the DeRidder story is why I'm here. I had a vacation coming, but Sam—that's my boss—couldn't justify sending me as one of the reporters for the Olympics—the ones with seniority got that. The sports people, of course. When I heard about Jackie, I went to Sam and said, 'Look, I know this woman; I went to school with her; she's from the same little area of North Georgia where I come from. Let me do an article covering another angle: a beautiful blonde woman married to one of the country's wealthiest benefactors. A man whose company gives millions to the Olympics, then just as he is about to enjoy all the sponsors' perks, his wife disappears into thin air. Or is taken.' I told Sam I feel she'll be located soon, so the second part of my story is bringing her back home."

He nodded thoughtfully. "Sounds like a good story, but I can't guarantee the part about getting her back home. This case is not as simple as it might appear."

"Do you think it's a kidnapping?"

He frowned. "We've been expecting a ransom call, but one hasn't come, for some strange reason. We're not ruling out the possibility of a carjacking."

"Tell me more." She leaned forward, her eyes wide, all her attention focused on Jay.

He reached for a piece of bread, dipped his knife in fresh butter, and seemed to double-check his answer. "You may be asking for privileged information."

"No, I'm not," she said teasingly. "I'm only asking for what's been available in the newspapers and newscasts. I'm just trying to catch up."

"As you probably know—" he took a bite of bread— "Jackie was last seen having lunch at Green Hills Country Club near here. She met her friend Merilee Champion, who tells us they had chicken salad and a glass of wine in the Oak Room. Then, Mrs. Champion went home to relieve the nanny. She left before Jackie, but the valet verifies Jackie left approximately thirty minutes later. She called her housekeeper from her cell phone to check messages. The housekeeper said there was nothing out of the ordinary about their conversation. Jackie was expected to drive home, change clothes, and meet her husband downtown at four o'clock for a special dinner before the opening ceremonies. She never went home, hasn't been heard from since."

"Were there any messages when she called her housekeeper?" Tracy asked.

"Nothing of importance. We've talked to everyone at the club. Nobody noticed anyone unusual loitering about. The valet brought her car around to her, and she drove off. That was the last time she was seen."

"Is it possible someone was hiding in the car?"

He sighed. "Anything is possible. We think it's more likely she stopped at a service station and someone forced their way into her car. But we haven't found a station attendant who can identify her. Another obstacle is the fact that her car hasn't turned up anywhere, and I can assure you there's a massive search underway."

She nodded, thinking it over. "Jay, what I'm having trouble visualizing is the Jackie I remember married to a man like Mr. DeRidder."

Jay nodded his head thoughtfully. "I know, but you see Jackie invested a lot of time and thought in improving herself. She worked her way through modeling school here in Atlanta, acquired some grace and charm, and took college courses in the evening. The Jackie of the jet set is totally different from the Jackie we knew."

"Hmmm." Tracy recalled the tall girl with a figure that was the envy of other girls, and the natural white-blonde hair. She sat in class, wearing bargain-store clothes, staring out the window, a dreamy expression in her wide blue eyes. "I guess she's another example of achieving the great American dream. I can see that she could evolve into a real beauty, and the self-improvement courses would level the playing field. But how did she manage to snag one of the richest men in Atlanta? A very prominent social type, at that."

Jay's broad shoulders lifted in a light shrug. "She was a member of one of his health clubs. They met at the juice bar one day. Maybe Jackie planned it that way." His lips tilted in a wry grin. "Who knows? Whatever the case, DeRidder seems to have fallen head over heels after twenty years with a very digni-fied wife. I suppose Jackie was just too tempting for a man bored with his marriage."

Tracy nodded. "Interesting. Did he divorce his wife to marry her?"

He frowned. "I think they were about to separate. Jackie just hastened the process. Once he became interested in her, Jackie focused all her attention on him, did everything she could to impress him. He was planning a business trip to France, so she took a crash course in French. He liked to ski in Aspen, so she took lessons. She didn't leave a stone unturned, apparently.

And she really spoiled him, in the beginning."

"The beginning?"

The server appeared with the tea pitcher, refilling their glasses. Tracy sat breathlessly waiting to hear more. The entire story fascinated her. She still couldn't believe the Jackie she remembered had accomplished so much in a relatively short period of time.

"According to gossip at the club," Jay continued, "she was seeing a tennis pro on the sly. We've investigated him thoroughly, thinking maybe there was a connection to her disappearance, but he has an airtight alibi." He sighed, glancing around the room before he lowered his voice. "Jackie was going out at night when DeRidder was in business meetings. Trying to protect her reputation is casting a shadow on the investigation. Still, I keep wondering if someone watched her from a bar stool some dark night and began to stalk her."

"So you think that might be what happened?"

Another little frown settled into the wide space between his brows. "The problem with that theory is that anyone watching her should have been noticed by someone. Particularly her. The people who seem to know her best say she never missed things like that, but she didn't mention anything."

"Was she seeing anyone other than the tennis pro?"

He shook his head. "Nobody that we've heard about. So we're back to the theory of a stalker, or maybe a carjacker. Since we're going into the fourth day and no ransom call has come in, we're beginning to wonder what the heck is going on."

They were both silent as they dug into their food, each lost in thoughts of the case. Tracy loved getting caught up in a story, and this one was more personal to her than any of the other stories she'd covered. Her imagination was spiraling, and her adrenaline had shifted into overdrive.

"All this while the Olympics are going on," she said, shaking her head in amazement as she thought about Jay's role in the case. "The people in your office must be pulling their hair out."

He grimaced. "Things are getting frantic. With all the tourists in town, not to mention the mix of nationalities and dialects, you can imagine the broad range of people we're dealing with."

Tracy shook her head. "Sounds crazy."

"It is." He looked at his watch. "Which reminds me, I'd better get going soon. I have to get back down to headquarters this evening to chase down a couple of leads on the DeRidder case that came in just as I was leaving."

"Oh." Tracy pushed back her plate and wiped her hands on her napkin. "Can I tag along?" she asked seriously, then laughed. "Just teasing. I'm finished, so we can go whenever you're ready."

"I don't want to rush you."

"You're not."

As he came around to help her from her chair, Tracy realized she had missed the old Southern charm of guys like Jay. In Moonglow, children were taught manners early and were expected never to veer from what they'd better have learned.

As she and Jay walked out of the restaurant into the soft, warm evening, darkness nestled like a gray stole over the broad streets of Buckhead.

"I'll follow you home," Jay offered.

"That isn't necessary, Jay. I'll be fine."

He winked down at her. "I don't doubt that you can take care of yourself. I want to see where you live. If I'm lucky, I'll see you again."

Tracy smiled. "Good. I'd like that."

After the valet brought her car around, Jay stood at the open door of the car, looking down at her.

"I'll be down at the media center in the Omni tomorrow

morning," Tracy said, smiling up at him. "Will you be in the area?" she asked.

"Depends. If I am, I'll look you up."

They smiled into each other's eyes, then he gently closed her door.

"Well, here's mine." He indicated the silver Ford the valet had parked behind Tracy's car.

"Good night."

She smiled again, watching him through the rearview mirror as he got into his car.

He doesn't look like an investigator, she thought, waving to him as she pulled away from the curb. Just looked like a great guy she'd like to go out with again.

He followed her to her driveway and did a wide U-turn before her house, then his Crown Victoria disappeared.

"Well, Tracy," she said to herself as she turned and walked inside, "this case is getting more interesting by the minute."

Six

J ay adjusted his rearview mirror and stared at the woman framed in the doorway of the cottage. He took a deep breath. He hadn't remembered her being so pretty or so interesting, and he hadn't expected to enjoy himself so much.

He reached for his car phone, remembering the urgent phone message when he had been beeped earlier. He knew he must act on the information he had received as soon as he could get Tracy home. Too bad he'd had to end the evening so quickly, but he was expected back at headquarters right away. Another body had been found...and there was always the chance that it was Jackie.

The heat soared to the mid-nineties on Tuesday morning when Tracy, wearing a sleeveless white blouse, a tan skort, and comfortable sneakers, rode the escalator up from the packed MARTA station and looked around, bewildered. A blaze of patriotic colors and Olympic rings greeted her in billboards, banners, T-shirts, caps, and pins, pins, pins. Everyone seemed to be trading or buying or giving pins away. The city was completely swathed in red, white, and blue. She felt like a civilian out of uniform at a military dress parade.

She wedged her way past jugglers and musicians, all of whom hoped to be "discovered" as they entertained those waiting for trains. Since she had needed every minute for grooming time, she had missed breakfast. Her hair was still damp on the ends from a quick shampoo, and yet she looked chic, as always. The natural waves along her crown gave her the appearance of having spent more time styling her hair than merely a few minutes with the blow-dryer and brush. She needed such an easy-care style, with her busy schedule. She wore light foundation, soft coral blush, and a light coral gloss across her lips. She had her morning ritual trimmed to thirty minutes, including the shower.

She fought back a desire to grab some toast and a cup of tea. Like so many other mornings in her life, breakfast would have to wait until coffee break or even lunch hour. In spite of a growling stomach, she was all energy and ambition.

On this day, many of the downtown streets were closed, but she had forced herself out of bed an hour earlier to board MARTA. She had made decent time. It was fifteen minutes after ten.

Sidestepping some playful college students, she made her way across the International Plaza, glancing up at the Omni, a tall building constructed of concrete, steel, and glass. It was a city beneath a roof, home to many of the Olympic events. It also housed one of the media centers, which was her destination this morning.

She thought of all the people and the events swirling within, and she felt her adrenaline soar. She couldn't believe she was here at the Olympics, part of history being made this week.

Amidst the mass of people, venues, and security officers,

she felt like an ant squashed beneath a roaring army of insects. She pushed through the crowds until she ended up at the offices of the frantic-looking news personnel. She was just beginning to reacquaint herself with some of the press when she spotted Jay, towering above the crowd. He was waving to her as he sidestepped clusters of reporters blocking his path. She waved back and met him halfway.

"Well, good morning," she smiled.

He was dressed in dark slacks and a white shirt. A silver badge gleamed from his belt, attracting an occasional glance from those rushing by. His dark hair contrasted with the white collar he was smoothing down as he glanced right to left. She could feel envious female eyes upon them.

"Hi." He smiled down at her, then glanced around at the melee taking place on all sides. "Got time for a quick sandwich?" he asked.

She heaved a sigh. "Man, do I! I'm all nerves and no nutrition. It took every ounce of willpower to bypass the coffee shop, but I felt I needed to get here first thing."

"Can you take a break now?"

"You bet."

His broad hand slipped around her elbow as he steered her back through the crowd.

"How did I get lucky enough to have lunch with you?" she asked, looking him over.

"Mr. DeRidder's office is over in the next block. I just came from there. Tell you about it later."

"I'm all ears," she said, excited by the possibility of breaking news.

Jay guided her around the shuffling crowd to the nearest fast-food shop. The hostess seemed to know him, and to Tracy's amazement they were seated at a table in record time.

"Whew. I see right now, I need to be your new best friend,"

Tracy laughed. "If I can tag along with you, my life will be far less complicated while I'm here."

It was a teasing statement, and she gave him a big grin to prove it, but his expression was doubtful. "You'd change your mind pretty fast. My life gets very complicated at times. For example, last night I had a message to come back to headquarters, that a woman's body had been found. And a blonde woman was at the morgue, but she had already been identified when I got there. It was not Jackie." He sighed.

"In any case, every day is a new complication in my line of work, and I think I'm headed for another one pretty soon."

"Can I ask what you mean by that enticing statement, or is it privileged information?"

A waitress interrupted their conversation, and it was not until their sandwiches were ordered that Tracy could pick up on Jay's tantalizing comment.

"Has there been a ransom call?" she asked quietly.

"Nope. Sorry." He studied her over his glass of Coke.

She pressed her lips together for a moment, trying to maintain her poise. Then she gave up. "You know, it'll drive me crazy to try and guess what's going on in the DeRidder case. You have what is known as a poker face when it comes to your work." She took a sip of her cold drink and felt instantly revived—though she wasn't sure it if it was the drink or Jay's sudden grin that had helped.

"Nothing is going on yet," he volunteered. "We're still chasing down every lead, that's all. At the moment, I'm waiting on one of the investigators to meet me here. He was across town, and I knew it would take him a few minutes. This was a good time to see you." His green eyes deepened, taking on a warm glow as he looked over her face. "You look very pretty."

"Jay," she laughed, "I know what you're doing but it won't work. I'm not vain enough to miss a change of subject when I hear one. So you're meeting your buddy. Then what?"

He nodded across the room, and Tracy shifted in her seat, spotting a short, heavyset man, midforties, stalking toward their table just as their sandwiches arrived.

"Hi, Bill. This is Tracy Kosell, a friend from Moonglow."

"Hi, Tracy." Bill gave a polite nod, then turned to Jay. "Ready to go?"

"Bill, I haven't had my hamburger." He indicated the fat sandwich being placed before him.

"Then bolt it down. We've got—" he glanced at Tracy and checked his words. "To get going," he said tersely. "This can't wait."

Tracy's breath caught. Had a ransom call come in? The bite of sandwich lodged in her throat. She couldn't swallow. An assignment always did this to her; she could count on nerves bringing a loss of at least five pounds.

Jay was gobbling down his hamburger, motioning to the waitress, who was engrossed in a conversation on the far side of the room.

"Let me get the check," Tracy offered. "Go on if you're in a hurry."

"Thanks." He stood, brushing his lips with a napkin. Bill was making shuffling sounds with his feet, reminding Tracy of a bull pawing the dirt, ready to charge.

"Tracy, I have tickets for the gymnastics event later," Jay said. "Want to go?"

"Of course I do! Where shall I meet you?"

He reached into his pocket, withdrew a ticket, and handed it to her. "At this seat in the Dome. Just go on in and find your place, if you don't mind. There's always a chance I won't make it, but I'll do my best." He drained his glass and turned to Bill.

"But…" She glanced from Jay to the ticket, then back at Jay. "See you there," she called after him.

He waved over his shoulder and walked off with his partner, who appeared ready to break into a run.

She stared after them, blinking. This was unbelievable. She couldn't have gotten closer to the investigation if she had planned it. What luck!

Turning back to her glass of iced Sprite, she smiled to herself. Maybe she was more than lucky, running into Jay again. Or was she? She frowned down at her drink, thinking of their lives. He lived in Atlanta, she lived in L.A. and loved it. Or did she? She felt herself being pulled back to the South, to her roots. She had always liked Jay as a friend. Now there seemed to be something more than friendship nagging at her each time she was with him.

She sighed, finishing her drink. She thought of the little dog she had adored and still missed since his death. He'd had a habit of grabbing her slipper to chew on, which led them into a tug of war. She felt a similar tug of war with her feelings now. Did she really want to stay in L.A. or come home? Did she want to get to know Jay better or avoid him as much as possible? If she wanted to remain neutral about their friendship, she couldn't keep seeing him. Yet…didn't she need him for her story?

Forcing her mind back to the day, she mentally composed a fax to send to Sam as she tried to concentrate on the case she had come here to cover.

Later, as Tracy stood in Centennial Olympic Park, gazing at the dancing water spouting from the Olympic rings, she tried to relax and enjoy herself. Children frolicked in the water while adults stood admiring the display. The moisture from the water cooled the air, a welcome contrast to the high humidity of the day. Her clothes practically stuck to her as the thermometer continued to climb to the upper nineties.

She turned and wandered back across the hundreds of thousands of inscribed bricks. For thirty-five dollars, one could get a brick inscribed with his or her name, forever immortalized on the walkway. She had been watching people locate the brick bearing their name when suddenly she looked down and there, at her feet, was a brick with the name *Jackie DeRidder.*

Tracy's mind flashed back to the last time she had seen Jackie. They had run into each another at a discount shop near Lenox Mall. Loaded down with packages, Jackie had almost bumped into Tracy.

"Hey, girl!" Jackie had called out. Her tone of voice was always warm and friendly. She was wearing her white-blonde hair very short on the sides and top—almost a boyish cut. Yet she looked very chic. The jeans and T-shirt were clean and savvy and fit her just right.

"Hi, Jackie. How are you?" Tracy asked.

"Exhausted. I'm working two jobs now, and I'm almost late for the first one. Hon, you take care." She had winked, then turned and made her way down the sidewalk. Tracy had stared after her, noting that males on the street were staring as well. Jackie had a way about her, a siren effect, even in jeans and a T-shirt. Once she'd been able to buy expensive clothes and dress in style, Tracy imagined she must have been stunning.

Tracy was still staring at the brick as her memory drifted back to the present. Looking at the name, she felt an inexplicable sense of danger. She wondered if Jackie had a chance to view her brick or if she would live to see it now. The chaos of the crowd rang through her ears, and despite the heat and humidity, she felt a chill of foreboding.

Would Jackie be found before it was too late? Or...was it already too late?

The thought depressed her. Wedging her way through the

crowd, she headed toward the Superstore, hoping to lighten her mood before she met Jay.

Tracy fidgeted in her seat at the Georgia Dome. She was one of thirty-two thousand spectators waiting for the women's gymnastics to begin. Jay's seat was still empty, but she was hopeful as she sat there, absorbing the electrifying excitement of the crowd waving flags and hoisting small banners. No American gymnastic team, men's or women's, had ever won a gold medal in a fully attended Olympic. She had a feeling history was going to be made.

Suddenly a roar went up around her, and she turned to see the American team marching in, all seven girls looking elegant and confident. A thrill of pride ran over her as her eyes moved from one girl to the other, each wearing her "game face." As they began warming up on the uneven bars, Tracy's eyes scanned the crowd. Jay was going to miss this. Where was he?

She recalled the tension in his partner's face. Had they found Jackie?

She forced herself to watch as the events began to unfold before her. Tracy had a good view from her seat in the center section; still, there was so much to watch, so many great gymnasts performing at the same time. She spotted world champion Lilia Podkopayeva of the Ukraine, graceful and smooth.

A figure moving in from the aisle caught her attention, and she spotted Jay apologetically sidestepping the feet and ducking beneath rapt faces attempting to watch four events at once. As he finally reached his seat and greeted her, Tracy nudged him.

"Hi. Nice of you to drop by."

"Thought I might as well." He grinned, reaching over to squeeze her hand.

She liked the feel of his broad hand against her small one.

Tracy found herself pondering a simple question: Why was she enjoying holding hands with Jay so much? Another part of her said, *Why try to analyze your feelings? Why not just enjoy the evening?*

She turned to Jay, smiling. "Thanks for inviting me," she whispered.

"My pleasure." He looked relaxed, and there was a glow in his eyes that had been missing at noon. *Probably the stress of his job,* she thought. Just to be safe, she refrained from asking him anything about his work. She glanced around at the crowd; many people were listening and pointing. One of the Russian girls had taken a fall, and now the U.S. team was in the lead.

Tracy sat mesmerized, watching the events as the crowd sat in breathless excitement followed by gasps and cheers and applause. The seven girls moved on to the beams, then to floor exercises, holding the crowd in spellbound fascination.

The girls on the U.S. team moved to the vaults. At first it seemed the U.S. team was in trouble. Tracy slipped to the edge of her seat, gripping Jay's hand tighter, as the taste of victory turned to fear when one of the gymnasts made two falls in succession. Then, on Kerri Strug's first attempt, she made her run, then fell, grimacing in pain. A few words from her coach, however, was all it took. She straightened her shoulders and went again.

She threw a strong vault and maintained her landing, extending her arms for the judges while lifting her left foot before collapsing in pain. As she was carried from the hall by her coach, her score flashed—9.712. The victory was clinched!

All of the girls had worked so hard, and now the look of pride and victory crossed their faces as they marched up to the podium to claim the gold. "Oh, Jay, look." Tracy pointed to Kerri, who was being carried by her stout coach, Bela, to accept the medals with her team.

Tracy swallowed hard, hearing a few muffled sobs around her. She had just witnessed Olympic history, and she turned to Jay, who looked touched as well. "This is wonderful," she said, gripping his arm.

His gaze met hers warmly. "Yeah, I'm glad we're here."

Staring at the U.S. gymnasts, Tracy realized how competitive she was. Was it this competitive spirit that drove her to be the very best reporter she could be? The thrill of victory, or being good at your work, was worth everything, it seemed to her.

Later, as they walked back to Jay's car where it was parked in a VIP area, he put a hand around her elbow and found his fingers tracing the two-inch scar there.

"Don't say anything about my tumble in the creek on that church trip to Tallulah Gorge when I was a graceful fourteen."

"Okay." Jay grinned, squeezing her elbow gently. "It was a long hike to Lake Tugalo, and the trail was rough, as I recall. It crossed several low ridges and narrow coves."

"You don't have to be nice. Besides, I was navigating just fine until we jumped a little doe and I was determined to take her picture. But when I lifted my camera, I got off balance on the rock and my foot slipped."

Jay was laughing harder now. "Sorry. I was just remembering how we all pitched in to dig you up out of the creek. The youth director wrapped his jacket around your bleeding elbow and headed out to the hospital with you. That pretty much ended our hike."

"Yeah, the cut only required a few stitches, but the fall ruined my camera. Never got that picture of the baby doe, either."

They laughed together and Jay sighed. "That was a fun place to go. Mom used to fry up chicken and make potato salad. Dad would pick a watermelon from the garden, and we'd load up the truck. Michael and I rode on top of all the gear in the back—always got into the fried chicken along the way. We'd head to the falls, and Dad and Michael and I would run trout lines at night. I remember one summer night we were frying fish at midnight."

Tracy smiled. "You have good family memories, don't you?"

Jay nodded. "The best."

She studied his features in the flashing neon of a sign they were passing on Peachtree. Those basic family values explained why Jay seemed so stable, she decided, so sure of himself, unlike her former love interest, Howie, product of three broken marriages.

"Hey." Jay squeezed her arm gently. "How about dinner?"

"I'd love to!"

"Let me make a quick phone call," he said as he opened the car door for her. Once she was settled into his car, he closed the door and hurried around to the driver's side, got in, and locked the door, then dialed a number on his cellular phone.

As he talked, Tracy watched the expression on his face turn from one of relaxed happiness to worry. When he hung up and turned back, he was already shaking his head. "Tracy, I'm sorry, but I'll have to offer a raincheck on that dinner. Something has come up."

"The DeRidder case?" she asked anxiously.

"Does it have to be the DeRidder case?" He looked at her, slightly exasperated. "I have others, you know."

Tracy said nothing, unsure of how to respond. Normally she was never at a loss for words, but this time an inner conflict raged. She was here to cover the DeRidder story, and she was getting nowhere. The man sitting next to her had the ability to help her, yet he was so loyal to his case that he remained close-mouthed.

61

"Actually," he said, taking a deep breath, as though trying to calm his frayed nerves, "a guy I've been searching for on a murder case has just been picked up." Her gasp brought a quick glance. "Sorry, but that's my life, I'm afraid. Anyway, this can't wait."

"I see."

They had shared a wonderful evening. Why spoil it now?

Jay put a tape in the player, but neither of them was able to relax as the soothing sounds filled the car. When finally they reached her driveway, he cut the engine and reached for her hand.

"Look, I have an idea. I haven't had an extra day off in weeks to compensate for all the evenings I've put in. What do you say to a drive up to the mountains and a picnic lunch tomorrow?"

Tracy stared at him, surprised by his invitation. "What about this emergency tonight? Won't it affect your work in the morning?"

"No, I'll wrap up my part of the paperwork this evening. That should entitle me to a day off. What do you say?"

Tracy thought it over. If there were a break in the DeRidder case, Jay would be the first one to know it. And if she were with him, so would she. Furthermore, she needed a day of relaxation, as well. "I say it sounds like a great idea. What can I bring?"

He shrugged. "Why don't we just stop off at that take-out place in Buckhead that specializes in picnic lunches? We can grab something on our way out of town."

Tracy laughed. "Sounds good to me. Look, you don't have to walk me to the door. I can see myself inside," she teased, hopping out of the car. She hesitated, looking through the open window. "Thanks for a great time."

"My pleasure. Pick you up at ten?"

"I'll be ready." She waved to him, then hurried across the

courtyard. She knew she had rushed through their good-bye in order to avoid a good-night kiss. Jay was making her uncomfortable, or she was making herself uncomfortable. Which was it? All she knew was that she should keep things on a friendly basis. There was no time or opportunity for anything more.

Seven

Precisely at ten the next morning Jay appeared at Tracy's doorway, dressed in Levi's and a black T-shirt. Tracy thought it was good to see him looking so relaxed.

"Great minds run on the same track," she laughed, indicating her black T-shirt and jeans.

"You look terrific." Jay grinned. "Ready to go?"

"Yep." She grabbed her shoulder bag and locked the door.

"According to the morning weather report, we're in for a slightly cooler day. Only upper eighties." He winked at her. "But at least there's no rain in the forecast."

They had crossed the courtyard and reached his car. As he unlocked the door, she glanced into the backseat and saw a picnic basket already waiting.

"You've picked up the goodies?" she asked, smiling.

"Couldn't wait to grab a muffin for breakfast. How about you?"

"I had a bowl of cereal. I think I'll resist those enticing smells until we get to a picnic site."

She saw his pager on the seat of the car, and then she glanced at the telephone. She hoped they could enjoy a simple picnic lunch without another interruption. What a hectic life it would be for the woman who got involved with him. And yet...

Her eyes drifted toward him as he started the engine and pulled smoothly away from the curb. He was such a nice guy, not to mention handsome. This morning his lean features were relaxed, and his eyes looked rested, even though he must have been up late with that murder case. She pressed her lips together, glancing back at the shops they were passing. She wasn't going to ask about the DeRidder case or any other; in fact, she had already decided not to mention work at all. It was the only way either of them could enjoy the day.

"I suddenly feel like a kid playing hooky from school," he laughed.

"Me, too! I almost feel guilty when I'm not stationed at that computer. So—" she smiled at him—"since we're both over-worked, we won't even mention the W word today."

"You've got a deal," he chuckled, grinning at her.

She sat mesmerized for a moment before dragging her gaze back to the entrance to the interstate. Yes, he was an attractive man, but if she were wise, she'd allow a pleasant friendship with him, nothing more. It would be a small miracle if they could get through the day without some reference to the DeRidder case. Still, she was determined to keep her mouth shut about it. She was certain he felt the same way.

They left Atlanta behind and relaxed with the Kenny G instrumental that had been in the tape deck the evening before. Tracy leaned her head back against the seat and took a deep breath, watching the highway climb higher. Time seemed to slip away as Jay's car zipped up the highway and turned onto a snakelike road that ran past orchards and vegetable gardens. Tracy watched the passing scenery, a relaxed sigh on her lips as willows, dogwoods, maples, and pines stretched before them.

Soon she was gazing at a mountain valley, rimmed by an emerald lake sparkling in the morning sun. Jay turned into the main gate leading to the spacious picnic grounds. They passed a couple seated at a picnic table, sharing a box of fried chicken. Further up, a family of four laughed together, munching on sandwiches. Jay pulled into the last space beside the lake, which seemed cozy and private.

"Well, let's see what surprises you have in that picnic basket." She grinned at him as he reached into the backseat for the basket.

"What do you say to peanut butter-and-jelly sandwiches?"

"I say fine." Tracy smiled, doubting that he had resorted to something so simple, and yet anything would taste good to her this morning.

He winked at her. "Then let's get out."

She hopped out of the car and put her hands on her hips, taking deep breaths of pine-scented air.

Jay placed the basket on the bench, then reached for a fallen pine branch to sweep the leaves and twigs from the table. Tracy busied herself hauling out paper plates and cups, and cans of cola, then arranging the potato chips and plastic-wrapped sandwiches.

"Maybe ham and cheese would be better than peanut butter and jelly," Jay said. "Or what about grilled-chicken sandwiches? I have one of each for you."

"Perfect. And I adore chocolate chip cookies," she said, admiring the large cookies she had spotted, wrapped in cellophane. "Thanks, Jay. This was really sweet."

"My pleasure," he said, swinging his long legs over the bench to sit down.

She took a seat opposite him. After years of being trained to say grace before a meal, it wasn't easy to shake the habit. But she wasn't about to voice a prayer with Jay in an open picnic area. Yet, he hesitated momentarily, closed his eyes, and offered a simple thank-you to God for this wonderful day.

She lowered her head, feeling a sudden pang in her heart. She was glad she hadn't avoided Jay. When had she ever met anyone quite like him? He was the perfect Southern gentleman and a Christian, as well. It occurred to her that Jay might have been heaven-sent to open her eyes to her own backsliding.

She glanced back at him, as though reassuring herself he was for real. He was eagerly unwrapping a sandwich. He reached for the canned colas, popped the top on each one, and poured them into containers of ice.

"You've thought of everything."

"Someone has," he chuckled. "I just found my way to the take-out shop."

He bit into the ham sandwich and closed his eyes, chewing slowly. Tracy thought he looked like someone who was relaxing for the first time in months, and she suspected this was true. He opened his eyes and glanced over his shoulder to the lake. "I can honestly say a charcoaled T-bone wouldn't taste any better."

"Since I never attempt to grill a steak myself, I have to agree."

"Oh, come on." He arched an eyebrow. "I'll bet there are plenty of guys willing to buy you a steak or lay one on the grill at their place."

"Actually—" she wrinkled her nose at him—"a guy served me one for breakfast a few mornings ago." She secretly delighted in the shocked expression that slipped over his features. "My dad," she said, bursting into laughter. "Steak and eggs, the works. My stomach went into shock, but he enjoyed cooking for me."

Jay nodded agreeably. "He's a great guy, isn't he?"

She shrugged. "If I must say so. We have our little differences. Mom always said we were similar in nature. Stubborn," she mouthed the word, then reached for her drink.

"You? Stubborn? And I always thought you were such a sweet little thing."

She took a cooling sip of her drink, then clucked disapprovingly. "Being called a sweet little thing is no longer a compliment to us liberated females."

"Are you a liberated female?"

She hesitated, knowing she had backed herself into a corner. "In some ways, yes; in some ways, no. But let's not get into anything deep here. I'm more interested in the scenery. Do you know how long it's been since I've picnicked?"

"Let me guess." Jay finished off one sandwich and reached for another. "Your last church picnic before you left home for college."

Tracy laughed. "Not that long. My last encounter with a picnic table was two years ago when I did a story on a charity event at a park in Santa Monica. But that gets into the subject of work, and we're not talking work today, remember?"

He shrugged. "Suits me, but that may get difficult. Let's talk about you. What do you do for fun in L.A.?"

"For fun?" she said, chewing slowly, thinking about it. "You know, Jay, I really haven't had fun in a while. This is the first fun thing I've done in a long time. Fun. Maybe I had to come home to be able to have fun. I think I've been too serious about...oops, don't want to mention that word."

"Then let's just eat."

"The perfect solution."

They ate in silence, listening to the distant laughter of children playing and birds chirping in the trees overhead. When finally Tracy wrapped the last half of her second sandwich and handed it to Jay, he shook his head. "Nope, why don't we put the rest of the food in the basket and take a walk?"

"I really do want that cookie," she said, laughing softly, "but not now."

As they placed the leftovers back in the basket and closed the lid, Jay reached for her hand. "Come on. It'll do us good to stretch our legs."

"We might need to break into a jog," she said lacing her fingers through his.

"Nah, let's be lazy."

Tracy stared at the path before them, littered with pine needles and an occasional pop can. Jay seemed so different today, away from the cares of his job. Her eyes drifted up at the sky, a pure blue with only a few baby clouds. She couldn't let herself read anything more than friendship into this as they walked along in companionable silence, holding hands, gazing out at the lake. Yet she felt a sense of pure joy that she could no longer deny. Being with him was a real pleasure, but it was like taking a turn down a dead-end street. Soon it had to end. *Don't think about it,* she told herself.

They crossed a wooden bridge that spanned the lake, and paused in the middle to watch a distant fisherman as he cast his line in search of a hungry trout.

"I'd like to go fishing sometime," she said.

"I'll be glad to take you. It's one of my favorite pastimes. I just seem to get interrupted every time...." His voice trailed off as he stared into space.

"Lake Lanier isn't far from Atlanta. You should be able to sneak up there fairly often."

He sighed and for the first time a frown marred his brow. "I haven't been up there since—"

"Since what?"

"Since Jackie disappeared. I went up there to escape all the crowd of opening day ceremonies."

"Oh," she said, then pressed her lips together. She had made herself a promise not to pepper him with questions, but for once he seemed to want to talk about the case.

"You know," he sighed, "life can get strange."

She stared at him. "What do you mean?"

He shrugged. "Just when I think I have things figured out, something comes along and trips me up."

What did he mean by that? "You asked about my life. Here's one for you. Where's the woman in your life? It's difficult to believe there isn't one."

His green eyes deepened as he looked down at her.

"There was for a while. It didn't work out." He picked up her hand, examining her fingers while looking thoughtful. "I guess I'm not too easy to get along with."

"Oh, I don't think it's your temperament. And you certainly know how to whip up a fine picnic lunch," she teased. She wanted to bring a smile back to his face, help him relax. He suddenly looked so serious, so worried. "Maybe there just isn't room in your life for a woman," she said softly.

"Honestly, there hasn't been," he admitted, lifting her hand to his lips, kissing her fingers.

Tracy stiffened. She couldn't let this progress beyond friendship. It just wouldn't work.

"Well—" she gently withdrew her hand—"I hate to end a wonderful picnic, but I'm hooked up for a conference call to Sam at two o'clock in Los Angeles. That's five here. And by the time we drive back to town...."

He stared into her eyes for a moment, saying nothing.

She knew he had read her signals, and maybe he agreed, for he began to nod. "Yeah, we'd better head back."

He took her arm, guiding her back across the planked bridge. "You asked about a woman in my life. What about you? Any special man in the picture?"

"Nope. Never a commitment."

"Why not? You have a lot to offer."

"I'm not very domestic, Jay. Aside from being outspoken and stubborn, I'm probably the worst cook you've ever met."

"Maybe it isn't important to you now."

She laughed. "It never has been. Mom did her best to give me cooking lessons, but I had better things to do. There was cheerleading practice and then journalism projects. Now I live on fast-food salads and take-out."

"Not being a gourmet cook wouldn't keep you from attracting the right guy."

She took a deep breath and looked up at the sky again. "To be honest, the right guy just never came along."

"Really?" He tilted his head to look down at her.

"That's right," she said as they reached the picnic table. "Now about those cookies...."

He laughed, opening the basket. As they munched cookies and threw their trash in the container, the relaxed mood returned. By the time they got into the car and drove off, both were laughing over a joke Jay had heard at work.

Half an hour out of Atlanta, Jay's car phone rang. He groaned. "I'm tempted not to answer."

"I'll pretend not to hear it," Tracy offered obligingly.

On the third ring, Jay gritted his teeth and grabbed it with a terse hello. The expression on his face changed instantly, and Tracy was aware that he was pressing the accelerator harder now. In fact, the speedometer registered eighty by the time he replaced the phone in its cradle.

"What's up?" she said, disturbed by the look of concern on his face.

"Maybe tomorrow I'll be able to tell you something. At the moment, there's nothing specific I can say. We may have a break in the case. I'll keep you posted."

Tracy sighed. "Do you have any idea how frustrating this is for me?"

"Sorry."

Neither spoke again as Jay concentrated on negotiating the car through the heavy Atlanta traffic once they reached the city limits. Tracy bit her lips, torn between curiosity and frustration. This wasn't fair. Why couldn't he tell her *something*?

"In the interest of time, do you want to just drop me off at the corner of the block?" She wanted her remark to come off as a flip sort of joke, but it sounded exactly like she felt. Sarcastic. Still, she didn't care. She was almost dizzy from the speed of their return.

He glanced at her and grinned. "Sorry, I'll slow down." As he pulled up to the curb, he leaned over, tilted her chin back, and planted a warm kiss on her lips. Her heart raced as the kiss ended, and for a moment they merely gazed into one another's eyes. Tracy couldn't say a word; she was still reeling from that kiss.

"I'll call you tomorrow," he said, squeezing her hand. "Where will you be?"

She took a deep breath, trying to pull her mind back to reality. "Where will I be?" she repeated, trying to suppress the curiosity that begged her to hound him for information. She had to be polite; otherwise, he would start avoiding her to keep from being grilled. "I'll probably be at home pounding away on my notebook computer. I'm doing some background information on our subject. By the way, can you give me the exact location of the house where she lives? I know it's on Tuxedo, but I couldn't decide which one."

"1317. Greek-Revival style behind brick walls and a wrought-iron gate."

"Thanks, Jay. I had a great time."

He squeezed her hand. "See you soon. Sorry to duck out like this but…"

"It's okay." She gave him a quick smile and got out of the car.

She closed the door to the cottage and stared vaguely at the window. She was still thinking about Jay, a man who seemed totally absorbed in his work. A man who had known since childhood he wanted to be in law enforcement. *What was so strange about that?* she asked herself. She had known she wanted to be in journalism and had begun her training as far back as high school.

Aside from a few brief and rather interesting relationships, there had not been a serious one. There had been Jason at CNN that first year she worked in Atlanta, but they had different backgrounds, different beliefs. And there was not the magic she wanted to feel. She had broken off with him and surprised herself by not really missing him at all.

"I should know better than to fall for a detective," she said into the silence of the room. But she was beginning to wonder if her warning was coming too late.

As Jay drove away, he wondered what Tracy would say if she knew the kidnapper might have just been caught. But there was no way he could have told her that. The body they had brought up out of the river last night was not Jackie DeRidder, and the search had heated up again today.

Now, according to Bill, at last there might be a break in the case. A ransom call had just been made to Martin DeRidder. Jay pressed the accelerator harder, and once he was out of Tracy's earshot he put the blue light on the dash of his car and turned on the siren as he sped through the city streets.

Eight

୬

While it was only eight in the morning, Tracy was already dressed and in her car. She had tossed and turned through the night, tormented over what Jay had heard in that phone conversation. She had also gotten into a row with Sam during the conference call about how little she had accomplished. When the word *picnic* slipped out, he made a choking sound.

"Tracy, you're there to work, remember?"

So today she was working. But how was she going to get a good look at Jackie's house if it was concealed behind a high wall? Tracy wondered, steering her car along the broad, tree-lined street where vast estates stretched behind brick walls.

She frowned. Turning a corner, she spotted the number, 1317, in a small brass plaque set into the brick wall. This was the DeRidder mansion.

Slowing down, she peered through the wrought-iron gate, glimpsing emerald lawns, a view of a flower garden, and then a sweeping brick structure with thick white columns.

She sighed. That was all she could see without parking in front of the house and drawing attention to herself. She glimpsed several cars parked in the circular drive, along with a uniformed policeman at the gate. Obviously, Martin DeRidder had beefed up his security in order to shield himself from the curious eyes of the public.

Her eyes swept the neighboring estate, a massive structure of Italian design. She shook her head. "Jackie, you came a long way, baby."

She drove on, lost in thought, trying to imagine a simple little girl from rural Moonglow ending up in this fabulous estate in Buckhead. But she hadn't really ended up here. Where was she now?

Whenever she became immersed in a story, Tracy always felt a deep fascination for the characters. What happened to Jackie when she left the club?

Consulting the city map on her seat, she decided to try her luck at the country club. She turned back onto West Paces Ferry and found Green Hills Country Club. Her eyes swept the huge, meticulously landscaped lawn and parking area as she guided her car up the driveway. The architecture of the club, with its quarried limestone exterior, reminded her of an old French country estate. The line of the building had a Norman flair.

She pulled up to the porte-cochere on the right and was greeted by a polite valet. "Can I help you, ma'am?"

"Yes, I have an appointment inside. I'm considering purchasing a membership."

It was a busy morning, and somewhere in the background a radio blared the latest reports from the Olympics. The swirl of confusion accounted for her good luck, she decided, as he asked nothing more of her but promptly opened her car door.

Handing him the keys, she stuffed a bill in his hand and headed up the stairs toward the front hall.

As she looked around and assessed her options, she noted

that the interior of the club was Old-World European. She located the ladies' room and darted inside. Her eyes roved over the golden fixtures at the sinks and lifted to the huge expanse of wall mirror. Checking her image there, she dug into her purse to touch up her lip gloss and dash a comb through her hair.

To her far left, two women dressed in Chanel suits with Pradi handbags complained of the service in the dining room today. She decided to get bold.

"Excuse me." She looked at the younger one with the friendly eyes. "Do you happen to know Jackie DeRidder?"

"Yes, I knew her," the younger one replied while the older one—probably her mother, Tracy decided—slipped a hand unobtrusively onto her arm. Tracy caught the slight pressure of the woman's hand and watched the younger one's face become more guarded.

"We really must be going, Shannon," the woman said, lifting her chin and looking past Tracy.

"Are you a reporter?" the younger one asked, looking her over curiously.

Tracy sighed. "As a matter of fact, I'm with the Associated Press. But Jackie and I went to school together and—"

"Young lady, we have nothing to say to you!" the older woman snapped, steering the younger one from the room.

Her luck did not improve with the hostess in the main dining room, or with the waitress, despite her generous tip. When it came to Jackie DeRidder, obviously everyone had been briefed: *Keep your mouth shut.* "No comment" was the order of the day throughout the club. At the valet station, she became freer with her money, mentally chastising herself for throwing around money she couldn't afford to loose. Finally, it paid off.

"Hal, over there, was on duty here Friday," one of the valets informed her. "He took care of Mrs. DeRidder's car. Hal?"

Tracy felt a surge of hope as a young man in his late twenties came bounding forward, an eager smile on his face as he greeted her.

Again, more money changed hands. She explained her mission briefly and got right to the point. "I'm not asking you to divulge any information or to put your job in jeopardy, but I just wondered about Mrs. DeRidder's mood when she left here."

He grinned. "She was having a good time. Got my best tip from her that day. She got in her Mercedes and headed out. No problem."

"And she was alone?"

"Yes, ma'am, she was alone."

"Any chance someone was in the trunk of the car?"

He looked insulted. "Not a chance. We have top security here; I can assure you of that."

She nodded. And yet she had proven her point. One did not have to be a member to get into the club or gather information. All it took was guts and some money spread in the right places.

Tracy made one last attempt as she spotted an older valet walking briskly toward them, a frown on his face.

"No one lurking about?"

"No one!" He stood feet apart, his stance and his tone defensive.

"Thank you very much." She smiled at him and hopped into her car. "Oh, did she turn right or left when she entered the street again?"

He shrugged. "I don't know. We were very busy that day."

She nodded. "Thanks again."

Tracy drove away wondering what sort of story she was going to write. She was getting nowhere, and she had no news that hadn't already *been* news.

Feeling frustrated, she decided to head back to her place and telephone Sam. He was always good for inspiration, particularly if he threatened to revoke her expense account for lack of a story.

Tracy sat at the kitchen table, staring at the blank screen of her computer. Her steno pad and half a dozen odd scribbled notes were stacked at her elbow, but nothing seemed to help. She couldn't believe she hadn't made a start on the story. Usually her fingers were twitching to get at the computer, to lay out the outline of her story. This time there was so much to cover, yet so much mystery and confusion surrounded the entire incident that she had no idea where to start.

She picked up the telephone and waited for the dial tone to be certain it was working. Why hadn't Jay called her? Replacing the phone, she fought a desire to call again and leave another message, deciding a lady has to have her pride.

She leaned back in the chair and let her eyes drift toward the window, forcing herself to think of other stories she had done. None was like this one. There was the story about Chad, a four-year-old who saved his mother's life by calling 911. And Alma, an eighty-year-old woman who fought a mugger for her purse and eventually won. The most puzzling story had concerned a string of mysterious thefts following parties in Beverly Hills. The cases were never solved, and Tracy had been intrigued.

Dozens more stories had come her way, none of which had been particularly outstanding, but she had found some satisfaction in doing them. Usually Sam's ideas. He was giving her more leeway now since she had proven she could get the job done. This story, however, would be her best one; a real coup if she could pull it off the way she wanted. She prayed Jackie would be found safe and sound in the coming days. That was the other half of her story.

She had three weeks here, counting accumulated sick leave and vacation time, and a few more days of generosity on Sam's part. Maybe if Jay had a lead, the case was about to break. Her eyes shot to the phone as she wondered again why he couldn't at least return her call. She had called the AP booth in the media center, but nobody seemed to know anything. Aside from the medals being won and features about participants in the Olympics, the main topic of news was still the crash of Flight 800. A memorial service had been held on Long Island to honor the victims and their families and friends. With tears streaming down her cheeks, Tracy had watched the television screen, her heart aching for the sad faces in the crowd.

But news of the DeRidder case was suddenly strangely quiet. Nothing seemed to be happening, and yet she had a gut feeling that something big was going on and due to Martin DeRidder's status, a lid had been clamped on everything.

The sun rays of early afternoon fell over her window. It was two o'clock, and Buckhead was quiet after the excitement of the bike races here yesterday. Tracy had spent a year in Atlanta before going to L.A., so she knew something about the city and its history. Buckhead was the Beverly Hills of the South, with designer shopping, excellent restaurants, and more than one hundred homes worth a million dollars. She would have to include that little tidbit in her story about Jackie DeRidder.

She typed: "Buckhead: So named because in 1838 Hardy Ivy mounted a buck's head on a tree over his crossroads store and tavern. This was the name the settlers gave the place and…" Her fingers stilled on the computer keys. What did that have to do with Jackie DeRidder?

She glanced toward the window, staring at a red petunia

peeking over the windowsill. What kind of life did Jackie DeRidder lead?

The DeRidder house. She thought again of the setting, formal and forbidding. She had tried to speculate about Jackie's luxurious lifestyle beyond the high brick walls, but she kept seeing the girl from Moonglow.

That was it! She *could* recapture that image; she did know something about that. She had the edge on the other reporters there, so she should be in Moonglow doing background on Jackie, not here, lost in a maze of what-ifs.

She scrambled over the mass of papers on the kitchen table, claiming the morning *Journal.* Before she dared head to her car, she had to know which streets were closed.

Flipping through the pages, she found the street closings and checked her map of Buckhead. Ah, the route she needed to take to the interstate was open today. Leaping to her feet, she headed upstairs to throw some clothes into her overnight bag.

Two hours later she turned off the main highway onto what was called Old Highway 441. Several years back, a new highway had been completed, running straight from Tallulah Falls north through Clayton and Dillard and into North Carolina. Most of the people in Moonglow had been relieved when the new highway bypassed them. Now, as Tracy drove through the quiet valley shaped like a crescent moon, she was glad, as well. Situated on the high banks of Rabun Creek in northeast Georgia's Rabun County, Moonglow was a picturesque little town beside a placid lake. Life flowed along at a comfortable pace.

She turned down Main Street, feeling her nerves relax—until she reached the red light where Jay was crossing the street!

Nine

❧

W hat?" she gasped. Then an idea hit her, and she pounded the steering wheel in frustration. *That was it!* The search had moved to Moonglow! Jay had known this and not told her.

She rolled down the window and stuck her head out. "Hi, *friend,*" she called sarcastically.

He stopped in the middle of the street, but this hardly caused a traffic jam in Moonglow. Olympic traffic had not stretched this far north, and nobody in Moonglow ever hurried anyway. It was the custom to allow all pedestrians the right of way, and that included all animals, as well.

Jay looked a bit sheepish as he spotted her and turned to walk toward her car.

"Hi, there."

"Thanks a lot!" she said, still amazed that he had been so secretive with her.

"For coming over to say hi?"

"You know what I mean. What are you doing in Moonglow?"

"Came to see my parents," he said, attempting to look serious. Tracy was not fooled.

"Sure, on a busy weekday you thought you'd just drop by Moonglow, which isn't exactly on your route to work, is it?"

He chuckled, glancing over his shoulder. "Bill will have my head for—"

"Not if I get a chance first. Jay, can't you give me just a little tip? I have nothing in the way of a story. Nothing!"

"And I could have nothing in the way of a job!"

The grin was gone from his face now as he looked down at her. The driver who'd pulled up behind her decided not to give them any longer for their middle-of-the-street chat and was leaning on the horn.

"Why don't you pull over to the curb there?" He pointed.

She wheeled in front of the ice-cream parlor and cut the engine. Shifting in her seat, she leaned against the steering wheel and waited for him to approach. Tapping her fingers against the wheel, her mind raced as she watched his long legs eat up the distance between them.

"Could I interest you in an ice-cream cone?" he asked as he reached her car.

"You certainly could," she sighed, reaching back for her purse. "I suppose Bill will have *my* head for stealing you away."

"Nah. He's talking with someone."

"Better be careful," she said, removing the keys from the ignition and hopping out beside him. "You could get as serious about your work as he is."

"Tracy, this is serious business," he said under his breath, his hand cupping her elbow.

"I know." She lowered her voice, as they stepped up on the curb and greeted passersby. "And I don't mean to make light of it. It's just that...." Her voice trailed off. She had no right to get mad at Jay for doing his job, part of which meant keeping his mouth shut on a case this big. Furthermore, she didn't want to stay mad at him. Being friends was so much better.

The bell over the door to the ice-cream parlor gave a merry jingle as they entered. Tracy looked around. The shop had changed little over the past two years. Peppermint-striped curtains and seat cushions created a wonderful atmosphere for white wrought-iron chairs and tables. A long, glass display unit held all sorts of tempting yogurts and ice creams with an assortment of toppings. The pink-and-white walls held several huge, colorful posters of the different flavors of ice creams and toppings. A gray-haired lady wearing a bright red sundress sat in the back with an adorable little girl of about six years of age. The girl's mouth was chocolate rimmed; she was definitely enjoying her huge cone of ice cream.

The only other customers were a couple of teenage girls leaning over the counter pointing toward their choices of ice cream. A stranger stood behind the counter, squashing ice cream down into waffle cones.

"What'll you have?" Jay asked as they approached the glass case and peered into gallons of tempting ice creams.

"Pralines and cream." Tracy smiled.

"Make that two," Jay said, reaching into his pockets for the change he had been nervously jingling.

"I'll grab some napkins and plastic spoons," she said, turning to the help-yourself counter.

She sat down at the table and waited for him to join her, taking the opportunity to look him over while his back was turned. He was dressed in a short-sleeved white cotton shirt with khaki pants and brown loafers. He looked as though he really had taken a day off to visit his parents, but she didn't believe it for a second.

"Don't tell me, let me guess," she said, taking a lick of ice cream from her cone while he sat down. She leaned close to him and whispered. "Jackie decided to chuck her fancy lifestyle in Atlanta and come home to Moonglow."

He rolled his eyes and looked at her. "You can do better than that."

"You're in Moonglow to check on a lead," she said more seriously, watching his face, trying to read his reaction. He kept the poker face while wiping his hands on a napkin. "That phone call to Mr. DeRidder brought you here." She leaned closer to him, whispering in his ear. She got a whiff of spicy aftershave and the scent of freshly shampooed hair. It was nice.

"I like the way you carry on a conversation." He tilted his head and looked down at her.

She swatted his shoulder and straightened in her chair. "You're impossible."

"And you might be getting warm with your ideas," he said. "But please don't ask me anything else, Tracy. This is too critical."

She knew she had to respect him for honoring the DeRidders' privacy, so she nodded and took a deep breath. What did she expect? He wasn't going to tell her anything. She realized it would be very unprofessional of him to go whispering to a reporter from L.A. But she wasn't just a reporter; they were supposed to be friends. She decided to try another approach.

"Okay, no more questions," she promised, hurrying through her cone. "You get to your work, and I'll get to mine. I'm on my way to Dad's house. Maybe I'll just interview some of her family while I'm up here."

"That's why you're here," he said, looking at her with obvious mistrust. "You know something."

Tracy tried to keep her expression calm. "Maybe I do, maybe I don't."

"You wouldn't leave Atlanta and come home for a visit in the middle of the week."

"That's my line," she quipped, finishing off her ice cream. "But I guess I'll just have to hint at what I've heard when I write my story."

"You'd better not do anything to endanger her life," he said under his breath. His eyes shot sudden sparks at her, and she caught her breath, amazed that he was so angry.

Tossing his napkin on the table, he came to his feet. "I think I'd better go. See you later, Tracy."

"But—" She gulped, struggling for words. She was at a complete loss as Jay turned and walked out of the shop.

Ten

Tracy opened the screen door and yelled hello. She could hear her father's voice from the spare bedroom, now converted to his office. He was probably on the phone with someone in his congregation, and with that in mind, she closed the screen door gently and started down the hall. She heard him say good-bye and hang up the phone. He poked his head from his office door.

"Hey there." His face held a surprised smile, and his eyes twinkled as she walked over to hug him. "Didn't expect you back until tomorrow. If then."

She gave him a peck on the cheek. "I couldn't stay away from Moonglow."

"Well, I'm glad to hear that. Come on back to the kitchen for some lemonade."

"I'll just put this in my room," she said, hurrying down the hall to set her suitcase inside the door. When she joined him in the kitchen, she began with the thought uppermost in her mind.

"Listen, Dad. I want to go to the cemetery and take some flowers."

He turned from the refrigerator, pitcher in hand. His brows arched in a look of surprise; then he gave her a gentle smile. "Sure. I go two or three times a week. We'll go late this afternoon when it cools down if you want to, or we can wait until the morning." He hesitated. "By the way, Beth wants to see you. She was hurt we didn't—"

"I know," Tracy cut in, then bit her tongue. "I'd like to see her too. And her family."

She knew she had to make her peace with everyone, especially Beth. But she wasn't looking forward to it. "Let me get a shower first and change clothes. I need to unwind a bit before we go."

"Sure. And I'll make some phone calls."

Later as Tracy and her dad stood before her mother's grave, she stared through a blur of tears to the bouquet of yellow roses she had just placed there. Her mother's favorite flower. It seemed so little to do, and her gesture of love had come so late. Pain swelled within her heart until she couldn't speak.

Her father was touching the tombstone gently. "She's in a wonderful place now, and we'll see her again."

And the first thing I'll do is apologize, Tracy thought, feeling the pain wash over her. And yet she could feel a tinge of relief in coming here, bringing flowers, standing with her dad, whose pain was evident as tears slipped down his cheeks.

Neither Tracy nor her father spoke on their return from the cemetery.

Her father's words were comforting, but Tracy still felt miserable inside. She had so many questions she wanted to ask, but she kept silent. Why had God allowed a good woman like her mother to go through so much pain? Why did drug addicts and thieves and rapists still walk the streets while she and her dad stood before her mother's grave? Why had her mother— her smiling, loving, godly mother—died at the age of fifty-five?

Eleven

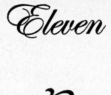

Jay sipped his coffee from a Styrofoam cup and thought back over the day. He hadn't meant to come off so sharp with Tracy, but she must have somehow gotten wind of what was going on, and that frustrated him. The last thing they needed in this case was a reporter snooping around. Particularly until the arrest was official.

"That about wraps it up for now," Bill said, hauling his short frame back to the car. He had overeaten at the local diner once he learned turnip greens and pork chops were the blue-plate special, and now his walk was little more than a waddle as he crossed the street to his parked car.

Jay followed. "I'll hang around here another day or so, ask questions. You know the drill." As he spoke, Jay stared down the main highway that led to the small town of Clayton. He was thinking of the husky little guy they'd just arrested, whose IQ probably wouldn't equal today's temperature. His last glance at Jay had been through the back window of a police car.

"I don't know about this guy, Jay."

Jay sighed. "Yeah, but if they think he's their man, let's give it a break. We haven't stopped in days."

"You staying with your folks tonight?"

Jay nodded, thinking of his parents' farm, seven miles outside of Moonglow, and the peace and serenity it offered. He couldn't wait to kick back in the swing on the back porch and watch Dad with his bird dogs. But first he had some apologizing to do. The sharp words he had spoken to Tracy still bothered him. And that was unusual, which made him think he was getting out of the safe zone in his feelings for her.

"Yeah, I'm staying," he said, finishing his coffee and tossing the cup into the nearest container beside the convenience store. "Why don't you go on back into Atlanta? How many questions can we ask? We've already checked things out. I'll make a trip up to Jackie's old farm—I know how to get there. That's all that's left to do. Head on back to town, man."

Bill released a deep sigh, as though all the cares of the past few days had been expanding within him. The whoosh from his chest sounded as though someone had just pierced a balloon.

"Think I'll take you up on that," he said at the end of that deep sigh. "You'll check out any other leads around here?"

"Yeah. In fact, I may stay all weekend. The guys can page me and tell me what they need."

Bill extended his hand. "We make a fair team, I reckon."

Jay shook his hand. "I think so."

Waving to Bill as he got into his car and drove off, Jay, too, breathed a sigh of relief. This case was more complicated than it appeared. Couldn't everyone see that? He needed to do some thinking...but first there was that apology to make.

Twelve

Someone was tapping on the screen door, and Tracy peered around the corner into the hall and saw Jay standing there. She couldn't have been more surprised.

"Hi," she said uncertainly, as she opened the door.

"Hi. Got a minute?" He looked serious, and yet a little grin played around his mouth.

"Sure. Want to come in?" She hurried down the hall.

"First, I want to apologize. I overreacted when we talked earlier. Guess I'm a bit tense."

She nodded. "I understand. I was only teasing, but I shouldn't have. I know your work is serious business."

He shoved his hands in his pockets, shrugging lightly. "We've been on this case practically twenty-four hours a day. Except for the picnic," he said with a grin. "I'm on my last nerve."

"Who's there?" her father called from the kitchen.

"It's Jay Calloway," she answered as Jay followed her down the hall.

Richard Kosell looked puzzled for a moment, but then he quickly extended his hand to Jay.

"Hello, Mr. Kosell," Jay said, shaking hands. "Hope I'm not barging in."

"Not at all. Good to see you, Jay." Her father appeared to take in stride the fact that first she, then Jay, had shown up out of the blue at his house. Nor did he appear surprised that she and Jay had become friends again.

Is that what we are? Tracy wondered, aware that her heart was beating faster as she watched Jay talk with her father about the Olympics. When their conversation reached a lull, Jay looked at Tracy and began to explain the day's events.

"You're going to see it on the evening news, so I'll tell you. An arrest has been made in the DeRidder case."

"What?"

"I think it may be a hoax. The guy is a drifter, trying to make some quick money, in my opinion. He only asked for a hundred thousand, and Mr. DeRidder could easily have paid ten times that amount. I was suspicious from the beginning. He did stupid things, hadn't thought through his moves." Jay sighed. "But it's out of my hands now. The FBI has taken over."

Tracy's dad was pouring lemonade and automatically handed Jay a glass. "Can you tell us more?" he asked.

"A ransom call did come in, as you suspected, Tracy. On his second phone call, we pinpointed his location—a pay phone near a convenience store in Clayton. The money was dropped off near a fast-food restaurant on the outskirts of Clayton. We just picked the guy up."

"A guy from Clayton?" She stared at Jay. "Fifteen minutes from here? That's incredible."

"He's pretty pathetic, actually. I'm afraid he has no idea where Jackie is, but I'm staying over to talk to some people."

Tracy was staring into space, thinking about what he had just told her. "This is incredible."

"And you don't think this man knows where Jackie is?" her father asked.

Jay shook his head. "I personally don't think so. I believe everyone involved in the investigation has the same feeling. He's just not smart enough to pull it off."

"What about an accomplice?"

"That's a likely possibility. If there is an accomplice, this guy will talk. He knows he's in big trouble, and he's scared."

Tracy scratched her head. "What a drastic turn of events."

No one spoke for a few minutes. Tracy's dad had been listening to the conversation, but when there was a lapse, he turned to Jay. "Tell me, Jay, how are your folks doing?"

"They're well. Dad stays busy at the service station. Mom's into her summer canning. I've promised to help Dad build a fence in the morning to keep the deer out of Mom's garden."

"Keep the deer out?" Tracy echoed. "Where's my camera? I could get some pictures after all."

"Come on out for a visit," Jay said.

Tracy smiled. His parents were really sweet people. She remembered an older brother. "Where is Michael now?"

"He's a detective for an insurance company, but he's hoping to start his own agency soon."

"Will you go to work with him?" Tracy asked, curious about Jay's plans. She was finding herself more interested in him all the time. He really was a nice guy.

"I'm happy with my job, so, no, I'm not planning to go into a private agency."

They had gathered around the kitchen table, and as Tracy watched Jay's eyes circle the cozy kitchen, she wondered what he was thinking.

"Reverend Kosell, I'm sorry about your wife," Jay said.

For a moment, Tracy felt as though a knife had just sliced

through her heart. She dropped her eyes to the lemonade, tracing a circle around the top of the glass.

"Thank you very much, Jay. We miss her. But she was ready to—"

"Are you two getting hungry? I am." The words bolted out of Tracy's mouth, surprising her as much as her father and Jay. She swallowed, wishing she could call back her frantic outburst. But she wasn't ready to talk about her mother. In fact, she couldn't bear even to think about her yet.

Her father quickly recovered and began to nod. "I've had a craving for some of Smoky's barbecue all day," her father answered smoothly. "Do you two want to drive out there?"

Tracy shifted in her seat, uncomfortable about putting Jay on the spot. "Jay may be in a hurry."

"As a matter of fact," Jay replied, grinning, "I can take the night off. Barbecue sounds great to me, and nobody barbecues like Smoky. Believe me, I've tried plenty of places in Atlanta."

"That settles it, then." Tracy came to her feet, almost kicking the chair over in her haste. "Coming, Dad?"

Her father hesitated, clearing his throat. "Why don't you two just bring me back a plate? I need to make some phone calls. Bill Ralston is going into the hospital for surgery on the weekend. He told us about it last night at prayer meeting."

Prayer meeting. Tracy stared into space, recalling the years of Wednesday nights when she had been herded toward the church, going to the church's Girls Auxiliary or choir practice or a special Bible study. Though she didn't always want to go, back then there had been a peace in her soul that was missing now.

"What about you? You want to go out to Smoky's?" Jay asked, looking at Tracy.

"Sure, why not?"

"I'm in no rush to eat; I had a late lunch. So you two take your time," Tracy's dad said agreeably. Tracy thought he looked pleased to have Jay around. Looking at him, it occurred to her that her father always seemed to know what to say and how to say it. She had forgotten how much she admired that quality in him.

"Okay, we'll see you later," Tracy said. As her father looked at her, she wondered what he would say to her if she voiced all the turmoil boiling in her heart regarding her mother.

Turning to Jay, she walked out of the kitchen, pushing her thoughts toward food.

Smoky's restaurant was located about a mile out of Moonglow at the junction of the Hiawassee Road. The restaurant was a concrete-block building, located a comfortable distance from the highway with plenty of parking space in front. The space, however, was rapidly filling up with pickup trucks and all varieties of cars. Hickory smoke from the outdoor pit floated on the hot summer breeze as Jay opened the car door for Tracy.

Smoky was hard at work spooning his famous sauce over at least a dozen slabs of ribs. "I just realized why people drive all the way from Atlanta to eat at Smoky's," Jay commented.

Tracy nodded. "Yep, if you like barbecue, this is the place."

Beneath a tall white chef's cap, Smoky's round face was a study in concentration as Jay and Tracy approached him. A chef's apron, bearing a few samples of dark red sauce, was draped over the cook's Levi's and T-shirt. Humming along with the guitar music drifting from within, Smoky was happy in his own world, oblivious to people coming and going.

"Hi, Smoky!" Jay clamped a hand on his shoulder.

Smoky's head swiveled. A wide smile flew over his face at the sight of Jay and Tracy. Smoky had been a football star in high school back in the sixties, and all of Moonglow and Rabun County were his friends.

"Hey, man." Laying down his long fork, he reached for a towel to wipe his fingers, then accepted Jay's extended hand. "How's it going? Tracy Kosell, haven't seen you since you took off your braces. What an improvement!" he teased.

"Hi, Smoky. Couldn't stay away from the best food in the world."

"You still living out in La-La land?" Smoky asked, as a grin crinkled the skin around his friendly blue eyes.

"Los Angeles is not so bad," she said defensively, "but it's good to be back in Moonglow."

"Your dad misses you," Smoky said, his smile fading. "I see him about once a week. He was here on Friday, matter of fact. Had a big take-out."

Tracy smiled. "He hasn't been missing any meals. And speaking of meals, we're going inside. It's torture, standing out here looking at those ribs."

Smoky laughed agreeably. "Go on in. Tell 'em I said to treat you right." He nudged Jay. "My waitresses can spot the heavy hitters. They'll bring you plenty of food."

Laughing, Jay and Tracy turned and entered the restaurant. Tracy's eyes ran over the wooden walls that provided a background for memorabilia: A hand-cranked telephone, a long-neck gourd, an assortment of crosscut saws. A painted mountain scene decorated one bucksaw.

The opposite wall was designed for those who could appreciate farming days—a wagon's doubletree, a saddle stirrup and curry comb, even an ox yolk. From the ceiling a size 12 Dutch oven dangled from a nail. A side table displayed a coffee grinder and a variety of old iron pots and pans and a few antique kitchen utensils.

A waitress breezed out from the kitchen, dressed in a baseball cap, T-shirt, and jeans. In a quiet corner, a young man strummed a guitar and began to sing an old familiar ballad. The singer's lilting voice settled over the crowd, and a few sentimental diners joined in.

Jay and Tracy slipped into the nearest booth as the smiling waitress spread huge menus before them.

Jay took a deep breath. "I think this is the first time I've relaxed all week."

Tracy nodded, trying to imagine all the long hours he had put in, covering Jackie's disappearance. "You must be exhausted with the strain of the investigation."

Jay shrugged. "Well, the FBI has been in on this case since Saturday night, but a lot has been expected of my team."

"I can imagine. And now what will you do?"

The waitress was back, pad in hand, pencil poised over the pad. Tracy turned blankly to the menu as Jay ordered a plate of barbecued pork with fried green tomatoes, sweet potato sticks, and coleslaw. "And a huge glass of your good tea," he added.

"Why not keep it simple? I'll have the same," Tracy said, closing her menu and glancing toward the singer, ending his music to a round of applause. Tracy didn't recognize a single person here, which only reminded her of the fact that she had been gone a long time.

"You asked what's next," Jay said, returning to the subject of his investigation.

Tracy was surprised. She figured he would be trying to avoid talking about his work, as he had before. Since their little spat in the ice-cream parlor, however, he seemed to be making an effort to be as congenial as possible.

"In my mind, we're back to square one, although some of the others may disagree." Jay frowned. "I just don't think this guy had anything to do with it."

"So...where is Jackie, do you think?" Tracy's eyes probed Jay's face, and for a moment they were both silent.

"To be honest, I have no idea."

The waitress was placing before them Mason jars of iced tea, with huge slices of lemon resting on the rim of the jars.

"I forgot to ask for unsweetened." Tracy frowned as she took a sip.

"You should remember that in Georgia, tea is always sweet unless you tell them different. Besides—" Jay's eyes flicked down her T-shirt and shorts—"you don't need to worry about your weight."

"Well...." Tracy took a sip of the luscious tea and decided it was a sin not to indulge in something as good as Georgia iced tea, exactly as it was meant to be sipped.

Smoky was making his way through the crowd, pausing here and there to offer a friendly greeting, tease a young couple, give an affectionate tap to an older man while inquiring about the man's health. Finally he arrived at their table just as the waitress delivered their plates. Smoky shot an inspective glance over the huge servings.

"Bring them a bowl of my fried okra," he quietly instructed the waitress, then turned to wink at Tracy. "Goes good with the tomatoes."

"Honestly, Smoky, if I lived here I'd have a real weight problem."

"Never," he chuckled, turning to Jay. "Saw you on the news the other night. Local boy made good."

Jay modestly shook his head. "Just doing my job."

"Yeah? Well, you must be doing your job right. I heard a while ago that some ol' boy up at Clayton had been arrested."

Jay nodded. "That's right. An arrest has been made."

"You know...." Smoky frowned, looking over his shoulder to see who was listening. He leaned closer. "I thought about giving you a call when I saw the news report that showed a picture of Jackie and her car."

Jay looked at him curiously. "Why were you going to call?"

"There was a black '96 Mercedes that whipped in here on Friday, but I couldn't see the woman's face, only the back of her head as she drove off. I asked the waitresses about her. One gal remembers a blonde woman got some barbecue to go. Didn't really notice her 'cause we were getting a large catered order together. I saved that write-up in the newspaper—the one with her picture in it? Nobody remembers seeing her here. But the gal who took her order is on a pack trip into the mountains. We can check with her when she gets back."

Tracy glanced at Jay thoughtfully and turned back to Smoky. "Did you notice if the car had an Atlanta license plate?"

"Nope. Just saw it from the side, and then my meat was burning on the grill. Had to turn back. We get a lot of fancy cars coming and going."

"I believe it," Jay said. "Your place is pretty famous."

"Anyway—" Smoky straightened, smoothing down his apron—"it probably wasn't her. Not with all that was going on in Atlanta that day."

Jay was silent for a moment, staring at his tea. "I don't think Jackie would have missed out on a cocktail party and opening ceremonies for the Olympics. And she'd have to do that to come up here that afternoon."

Tracy knew Jay was right, yet as a journalist, she was always pushing. "Smoky, are you sure there was nobody with the woman you saw?"

Smoky nodded. "Yep, I'm sure the woman was alone."

Tracy frowned. "Do you remember Jackie?"

"Nope, you know those folks lived up Yellow Creek Cove just on the other side of Moonglow. Wasn't the man a logger before he got killed?"

Jay nodded. "Jackie's parents were killed in a car wreck years ago."

"Hey!" Smoky glanced at their plates of food. "Don't let me

slow you down." He tapped Jay on the shoulder. "What do you think of my barbecue?"

"Better than ever." Jay grinned, going after another bite.

"And what about you, Miss L.A.?" Smoky teased.

"Your famous barbecue is even better than I remember. In fact, could you fix up a plate for Dad? This was his idea."

"Sure thing. Reverend Kosell always gets the best," he said over his shoulder, bounding off toward the kitchen.

"I have a feeling everyone gets the best," Tracy said as her eyes followed Smoky.

"I think so," Jay agreed. He studied her quietly over his tea glass.

Tracy wiped the barbecue sauce from her mouth. "Jay, I'm sorry if I've pushed you about the investigation for the sake of my story. Pretty selfish, huh?"

"You're doing your job like I'm doing mine. So what kind of story are you going to write? Be careful what you say about the guy we've arrested. We haven't proven anything yet."

Tracy nodded. She was having more difficulty with this story than any she had ever tried to write. "I think I'll have to change the focus. Let it be more about the little hometown girl who made good, who got everything she wanted but—"

"But it wasn't enough. Are you going to put that in?"

She sighed, studying her food. "In fairness to her, I can't write that, although it certainly seems that way, doesn't it? I guess I'll just write about Moonglow and her life here, then the stark contrast of life with Martin DeRidder. And, of course, I'll highlight some of the things he's done for Atlanta."

Jay nodded. "He's done a lot of good. Actually, he's a very nice man."

Tracy leaned forward. "Do you think there's a chance that I could interview him?"

"I doubt it. He isn't talking to anyone. Her security is still at risk, you know. Until we have some idea...." His voice trailed off as he quietly finished his food.

"I know, and I don't mean to be insensitive. I'll come up with a story. I always do."

"You really like your work, huh?"

The waitress appeared with the bill, glancing at the Olympic T-shirt Tracy had bought in the Superstore.

"You get a discount on your meal," she said with a wide smile.

Tracy glanced down at her T-shirt. "Because I'm wearing an Olympic shirt?"

"Not just that." She lifted her pencil to indicate a sign in the rear, advertising a discount on meals for all who wore baseball caps or T-shirts.

Jay laughed. "I'd forgotten that."

Tracy's eyes scanned the room. Everyone looked relaxed and comfortable. Maybe that was the idea behind Smoky's sign—that and the fact that jeans, a T-shirt, and baseball cap was his favorite attire when not wearing an apron and tending the barbecue grill.

As Jay paid their bill and waved to Smoky, Tracy accepted the carton containing her father's order. "I'll be glad to pay for mine and Dad's," she offered.

"Nope, you paid for our last meal."

"I did?"

"The coffee shop Tuesday. And I know what the prices are downtown, with the Olympics and all."

She shrugged. "It wasn't that bad."

The guitar player had returned from his break and was now strumming "Dixie" to an appreciative audience. It left Tracy with a nice feeling as she and Jay walked back to the car in the growing darkness.

"Tracy, what are you doing this weekend?" Jay asked, his

hand on her elbow as they crossed the gravel parking lot to his car.

She took a deep breath. "I hadn't thought about it, to be perfectly honest. But I'll probably stay in Moonglow, talk to some people. I brought my laptop computer and my notes, and I do a lot of business by phone, anyway."

He nodded. "Look, unless I get a call to return, I'm staying over until Sunday afternoon. Remember Tommy Woodfin? He's having a cookout at his farm tomorrow evening. It's the letter-man's reunion. Lettermen from high school," he elaborated.

"Oh." Tracy nodded, thinking about Jay's football team. Moonglow had won the state championship the year he graduated.

"Every year we have a reunion in July," Jay was saying, "and the guys plan for months, bring their wives and friends. This is Tommy's year to host it."

"Okay, sounds like fun." Tracy thought back to high school, recalling Tommy Woodfin, the big middle linebacker who had been the toughest guy in school. "Is he still married to Lisa?"

"Nope, they split up a couple of years ago. Anyway, it will be a chance for you to see some of the people from high school, even though everyone is older than you."

"But I'm so mature," she teased, sliding into the front seat of his car while he held the door.

His eyes ran down her T-shirt and shorts, lingering on her suntanned legs. "Yep," he said, closing her door.

As she watched him walk around the car, she remembered his football team and chided herself for not asking about his role in their winning so many games that year.

"I remember you were a very good running back," she said as he got in.

"Only in high school," he said, cranking the engine. "I never made it in college."

"Well, that's okay. Who said you had to?"

He laughed. "Nobody, thank God." He placed his hand on the back of the seat and glanced back to check the traffic as he backed the car out.

Tracy's eyes drifted back to the little barbecue restaurant, where the sound of pleasant voices and guitar music filled the summer evening.

"You know, I really have missed this down-home attitude. It's been so long since I went to a restaurant and had the owner come out of the kitchen to talk to me. Or my companion," she said, nudging Jay.

"And we've missed you. Ever think about coming back?"

The question took her by surprise. She looked across at Jay as he guided the car back onto the highway. "Actually, I have considered coming home at times, but I always figured I would be bored here now. Not that it isn't a wonderful place...."

"I understand." He turned down the music on the radio and glanced at her. "Could I ask you something?"

"Sure, go ahead."

He hesitated, obviously unsure of how to phrase his question.

"Well, what is it?" she prompted, expecting to hear something about life in L.A. or her work for Associated Press.

"You don't seem to be comfortable talking about your mother," he finally answered. "Maybe I shouldn't mention it."

Her eyes shot to the highway as she studied the yellow line curving along the center of the road. "It was very upsetting," she said quietly. "I couldn't be here during her illness, and I always felt it was expected of me."

"Why? You lived and worked a long way from here."

"I know but...." She swallowed hard. "It isn't just that."

"You wanted to be here, but you couldn't. Don't be hard on yourself."

"No," she said weakly, hardly able to speak. "I *didn't* want to be here. That was the problem. You see, it hurt me so much to see the blank stare in her eyes, to know that she didn't even recognize me. I guess I was in denial at first; then when the truth hit, I just couldn't deal with it."

Tracy could feel the tenseness stretching her nerves taut; sometimes she felt like a rubber band, ready to snap. She heard the rasp to her throat, and she was grateful that Jay was sensitive enough to realize she was unable to talk about her mother for long. He had glanced quickly at her, then looked back at the street as he turned into the quiet neighborhood where her father lived.

In the soft semidarkness, the houses sat back from the street, sheltered by large oaks and neat green yards. It was the kind of setting modern homeowners tried to duplicate but never quite attained. The gentle aging of trees and homes was always missing, and Tracy thought that added charm. Broad front porches held chairs and rockers, and here and there bikes were casually parked. Even an occasional toy was left out in the yard. Obviously, no one considered theft because it was rare in a town where folks respected one another's property. She had always loved this street, but now as she drove back to the house where she had lived for so long, she felt the weight of the past settle over her. The grief inside was like an ache that stretched throughout her body, and as she looked at the neighborhood she had once loved so much, there seemed to be something terribly wrong with this picture. And she knew what it was: Her mother, who had been so vital to the community, was gone. It felt as though there were a huge hole inside of her. She took a deep breath and closed her eyes.

She turned back to Jay, trying to thrust aside this awful sadness as she thought of his going home, visiting with his mother and father. In a way, she envied him the chance to return to his mom.

She cleared her throat. "I hope you have a good visit with your parents tomorrow."

He pulled smoothly into her driveway, then turned back to her, the engine still running. "Thanks, I'm sure I will. The cook-out starts at six. Shall I pick you up then?"

"Sure. I'm going to spend some time with Dad," she said, glancing up at the porch light. He still left the light on for his girls, a beacon in the night. "And I'll be forced—" She bit her lip. "I mean, I'll be seeing my sister and her family," she amended.

"Then enjoy yourself. And thanks for a good evening."

His arm had been on the back of her seat, but now his hand touched her shoulder, and he leaned forward, planting a kiss on her lips.

The touch of his lips and the expression in his eyes unsettled her. Her heart beat faster as she looked at him. She gripped the Styrofoam carton of barbecue tightly.

"Well," she said lightly, "Dad will be starving. I'll see you tomorrow. And you don't need to walk me to the door," she laughed, getting out of the car.

"If you say so."

She slammed the car door and waved again, then stood in the driveway, watching his car disappear into the night. It occurred to her that she didn't feel like a reporter who flew back home to do a story. She felt like a teenager again, back in Moonglow, and the thought was as warm and sweet as the smell of the hickory smoke floating up from the barbecue in her hand.

She thought, as she entered the house, that it felt good to be coming home, but there was a lingering sadness as well because her mother was gone. She turned toward her father's office, hearing his voice there. When she appeared in the doorway, she saw him seated at his desk, speaking in a gentle voice to someone who obviously needed counseling. She held the carton up to him, and he nodded, motioning to her to take it to the kitchen.

She turned back to the hall. Her dad worked hard as a minister yet barely earned enough to make ends meet. Somehow that didn't seem to matter to him.

She made her way down the hall to the dark kitchen and flipped on the light switch. The light flowed over the kitchen, reminding her there was no one here to greet her, no baked surprise awaiting her return. Tears welled in her eyes. *Mom, I miss you so much.*

Thirteen

Have another biscuit, Jay."

His mother had already plied him with sausage patties, eggs, grits, gravy, and two of her huge, fluffy biscuits. Now another serving of fresh hot biscuits was being added to the heap.

"Mom, you're killing me," Jay teased, holding his stomach.

"Ah, come on," his father scolded from the other end of the table. "I'll bet you don't eat right living in town and staying on the run."

Jay looked down the table to his father, a rotund fifty-eight-year-old man whose forty years of mechanic work was etched in the lines of his face and the brawny arms. He was tall, with hair that was still thick and dark, peppered with gray on the sides. On this Saturday morning, he wore work clothes because Mike Calloway always worked, whether it was at home or at his service station. His dark eyes glowed with the prospect of starting another project, particularly with his youngest son to help him.

Jay glanced toward the kitchen stove. "Mom, why don't you take a seat and enjoy your food? You've hopped up and down half a dozen times." He glanced at the small helpings of food on her plate, scarcely touched.

"I'm coming," she called merrily. She, too, was a bit over-weight, but because she was tall and large framed, she carried her weight well. She wore her brown hair in a short perm, and she dressed in Levi's and shirts. Other than hazel eyes, her features were a replica of Jay's. It was Jay's older brother, Michael, who looked like his father, except both had his height, well over six feet.

"Ellie, bring over some of that muscadine jelly you been hoarding for Jay."

Her merry laughter rang through the kitchen. "I almost forgot it." She rushed to the refrigerator and removed a jar from the back of the second shelf. "And I haven't been hoarding it, Mike!"

They exchanged warm smiles, assuring Jay that, as usual, their bickering was all in fun. After all these years, they were still crazy about each other.

She placed the jar on the table and took her seat, capturing Jay's free hand with her own. "We got a new pastor at church. Can you stay over and come with us?"

He grinned. "Sure. I've missed going to church with you. Sundays never go right for me when I don't recharge my battery with God's Word. I'm not planning to go back until Sunday afternoon." He plastered a hot biscuit with the clear red jelly. "Speaking of pastors, Tracy Kosell is home for a visit. You remember her?"

"Oh, that cute little girl!" Ellie's hazel eyes twinkled. "'Course I remember her. You been seeing her?" A grin played over her wide mouth.

"Sort of. She's a reporter from the Associated Press, now living in Los Angeles."

Mike groaned from the opposite end of the table. He took

great pride in never having been out to "hippie" country. It was a phrase he had clung to since he was Jay's age.

"She's covering the DeRidder story."

Ellie's smile faded. "That's so sad. And you said you don't believe this guy from Clayton is the real kidnapper?"

Jay sighed, suddenly losing his appetite.

"For heaven's sakes, Ellie. Let him alone about that blasted case. He came up here to forget, not to be hounded about it."

"I'm not hounding him," she bristled, glaring at her husband.

"It's okay, Mom." Jay reached over to give her a kiss on the cheek. "This breakfast is wonderful. Will building that fence around your vegetable garden make you happy?"

Her eyes lit up again. "Just having you home for the weekend makes me happy. But yes, I'll be relieved to keep those animals out. You know they nibbled down my azaleas this spring when Dad and I went fishing."

"Sorry." Jay winked at her.

"Well—" Mike was pushing back from the table—"I've bought enough chicken wire to surround every individual plant if we need to. Ready to get at it, Jay?"

"I'd better get at it," he said, finishing the food on his plate and pushing the plate back. "If I eat another bite, I won't be able to bend over."

Ellie laughed with delight. She loved to see her sons well fed.

"Jay, have you talked to Michael lately?"

He frowned. "Nope." He hoped she wouldn't start asking questions about the state of Michael's marriage. He knew that Michael and Elizabeth had separated, and little Katie was torn between the two. He just hoped his mom didn't know that.

"I get this feeling that things aren't right." Ellie frowned. "You know how mothers get these instinctive feelings."

Mike was frowning down at her. "That Elizabeth is too independent. Just because she inherited that plantation house doesn't mean they've got to up and move out there, especially since Michael's work is in town."

"Dad, you're a good one to talk about living in town," Jay teased, following him out the back door.

"You couldn't hogtie him and drag him into a city house," Ellie yelled after them.

Jay chuckled as they made their way down the steps of the back porch and headed across the backyard. It was a small farm with plenty of woods surrounding the land, and Jay had great memories of the place. "Dad, how long do you think it'll take us to build that fence?" Jay asked. He was already thinking of the party this afternoon and the fact that he would be seeing Tracy again. He seemed to be thinking of her constantly, and that worried him. This relationship couldn't work. Hadn't she indicated she wasn't interested in living here again? And he was married to his job. He couldn't see how they could work anything out, given the circumstances. The thought was like a weight on his heart, but then his father spoke, turning his attention back to the subject at hand.

"Oh, I reckon we can knock this project out in a few hours."

Jay nodded, unbuttoning the waistband of his jeans. He had eaten so much he was almost sick, but he didn't want to offend his mother. And not filling your plate and then emptying it would definitely offend Ellie Calloway.

Fourteen

Tracy awakened with a sense of dread. Her head rolled on the pillow as her mind drifted from half sleep to full consciousness. What was there about today that...

She groaned, snuggling deeper under the sheets. Today she and Dad were going to Beth's house for lunch.

She clenched her eyes together, ashamed of herself but unable to stop the dark feelings of grief and guilt that swept over her like a tidal wave. The only way to deal with this thing was head-on, and it was time she did that. She had pushed family problems to the back burner of her mind for as long as possible.

Slowly, she sat up in bed, sniffing the air. She could smell bacon frying and her stomach growled. Tossing back the covers, she pushed her feet into her flip-flops, reached for the silk robe that matched her pajamas, and headed for the shower.

Later, as she sat at the breakfast table with her father, she bowed her head and listened to his prayer. The guilt that had been nagging surfaced again. She was ashamed of herself, and sometimes she was ashamed of God for allowing her mother to die in such a horrible way. As they began eating, she lapsed into silence.

"Beth is expecting us at twelve," her father announced. "Ken is going to grill pork chops."

Tracy nodded. "They're happy together, aren't they?"

Her father glanced up from his eggs. "They seem to be. Ken is a good husband and a wonderful father."

"And, of course, Beth is perfect." The words tumbled out before she could stop them. She sank her teeth into her bottom lip, dropping her eyes to her plate. "Sorry. I don't know what's wrong with me."

"Of course you do." Her father leveled a stern gaze across the table. "You resent Beth; you always have. And now that she's happily married with a home and family—"

"Which is more than I have, you're thinking."

"You don't know what I'm thinking." Her father's face was tense now, and his neck was getting red as it did when he attempted to deal with anger.

"Oh, but I do!" Tracy threw her napkin down. "Beth spoke for everyone when she said I ran when things got rough here. *Ran out,* as though I lived down the street. Naturally, Beth can't relate to the price of plane fare back and forth or the expense of driving from California to Georgia. She went from being supported by you to being supported by Ken. She's locked away in her perfect little world and—" She forced herself to shut off her angry words. Dropping her head to her plate, she felt the tears rush to her eyes, and now there was no stopping them.

"Tracy, we've forgiven you. Why can't you forgive us?" her father asked quietly.

"Have you forgiven me, Dad?" She raised her eyes slowly to her father, seeing him through a blur of tears. "You've been put on a pedestal by everyone; you can't allow bitterness or blame

116

to show, but I know you are bitter toward me for not coming home more. I know you are," she said brokenly, as the tears flowed down her cheeks.

"All right, I'll admit it. What I felt was not so much anger as hurt that you didn't come to visit your mother toward the end. If there was any anger in my attitude, it was for *her*. She asked for you."

"Stop it!" Tracy sobbed, jumping up from her chair. "Please, just don't say any more."

She stumbled from the kitchen to her bedroom, her stomach heaving, her heart breaking. She couldn't bear to think of her mother calling for her, wanting to see her, while her youngest daughter had fled from the ravaged face and body of a woman who hadn't recognized her in months. Most of the time, she didn't even recognize her husband of thirty-five years.

She fell over her unmade bed, sobbing into her pillow, hating herself already for the words she had spoken, hating herself even more for the coward she had become in dealing with the horrible disease of Alzheimer's.

She heard slow heavy steps entering the room, and soon she felt a heavy hand gently stroking her shoulders.

"Please, honey, don't cry. You're only human. We're all human. I was bitter; Beth was angry; you were in denial. But, sweetheart, you need to deal with your emotions. You need to come to terms with what you're feeling."

She nodded, her face buried in the wet pillow, her stomach still heaving. She just knew she was going to lose her breakfast any minute.

"Can't we just start with today, with now, and go on?" her father suggested. His voice sounded gentle and tender, as though he were counseling someone in his congregation. Some part of her brain argued that maybe that was exactly what he was doing, transferring himself from father to counselor and bypassing some of his own pain.

"I want to start over," Tracy sighed, wiping her face. "But I don't think anyone else is willing to let go of my neglect. Beth handled Mom's illness so well, just like she handles everything else." She turned her head toward the wall, away from her father, as she took another swipe at her face with the back of her hand. "I'm sorry I've been such a disappointment."

"Tracy, don't ever say that again. Your mother and I were very proud of you. Just as proud as we ever were of Beth. But you seem to think...." His voice trailed off as he sat down on the bed and heaved a weary sigh. He sat with his back to her, his shoulders slumped forward.

Sensing the burden he carried, Tracy felt a slap of guilt to her emotions, along with a wave of revulsion. Toward herself.

"Tracy, don't you want Beth to be happy?" her father asked finally, glancing over his shoulder.

She swallowed hard. "Of course I do! You know I want Beth to be happy. It's just that...." What could she say? How could she analyze her feelings when everything had become so complicated?

"You have this idea that your mother and I thought your sister was perfect and that you were a rebel," her father said quietly. "Isn't that right?"

A smile wobbled on her lips. "I *was* a rebel," she admitted.

"Yes, you were. But you know something? Your mother and I always admired your ambition, your boundless energy, your drive. I'm sorry if we gave you any other impression. Naturally, I'm grateful for Beth and her family and the fact that she chose to stay in Moonglow. But that takes nothing away from you. Please understand that, if you understand nothing else."

Her eyes locked with her father's. She tried to find her voice to respond, but her throat seemed to be paralyzed.

"If anyone is being critical of you, it's you," he said gently.

The telephone made a shrill sound in the tense silence, and Tracy jumped.

"Excuse me," her father said, getting up and heading for his office.

Tracy dragged herself up from the bed, reaching for a Kleenex in the box on the nightstand. Wiping her face, she took a deep, long breath and tried to regain her composure. She hadn't let her emotions get the best of her in a long time. To her amazement, she felt better, even though she had spoken some bitter words to her father. She'd make up for it. Somehow she would.

Her father was talking in a low voice in his office as she crossed the hall to the kitchen. For several seconds, she stood in the center of the kitchen, looking around the room where her mother had spent so much of her life. She walked over to the counter, running a hand over the tile countertops that her mother had so patiently cleaned, hundreds of times. Her eyes drifted to the electric stove, to the burners in need of her mother's patient cleaning. She would do that before she left. Staring at the burners, she remembered her mother frying chicken there. On that summer day, two years ago. Beth had called Tracy aside to whisper about her mother forgetting important things, losing her keys, giving up her Sunday school class after going blank in the middle of her lessons.

"Beth, she's stressed out. Nothing more," Tracy had defended. "Give her a break."

Then that afternoon, her mother had turned blank eyes to Tracy and said, "How about fried chicken for dinner tonight? Would you like to have fried chicken?"

"Again?" Tracy quipped, thinking her mother was joking. After all, they had cleaned up the skillets from fried chicken only a few hours before. Then, with a sinking heart, she saw that her mother was perfectly serious.

"Again…" her mother repeated, staring into space. Tracy could see her mother trying to make the mental journey back to her last meal…and failing to get there.

After Tracy returned to Los Angeles, her father had called and told her in a sorrowful voice that he had had to restrict her mother's driving. She had gotten lost coming home from the grocery store twice in the past week. And she was no longer attending church regularly because she couldn't remember the names of people in the congregation.

The doctor had told them that the disease had progressed rapidly, even though fifty-three was young for a woman to get Alzheimer's. Still, he had spoken of the progressing illness as though this were a blessing, and Tracy had never understood the real implications. Then, one of her coworkers had told about her grandmother having Alzheimer's. Of being in a nursing home, totally helpless, for years. At least her mother had not endured the ravaging illness that long. Two heartbreaking years had been long enough.

Wearily, Tracy picked up the dirty plates and silverware. She'd clean up the kitchen, and then they could get on with the day's dreary business. In the background, she could hear her father's voice, patiently explaining a verse of Scripture to someone on the phone. What a demanding job he had!

"He's on call twenty-four hours a day," her mother had once said to her. "We have to share him with his congregation." But her mother had never seemed to mind that; she had considered her life a calling, as well. And Tracy had always known that being a minister's wife was a definite calling.

"Mom, I could never be in your shoes," Tracy had said to her mother, on many occasions.

"You'll make your own path, darling. And you'll fill your own shoes in your own way." Her mother had spoken tenderly, giving her a quick peck on the cheek to emphasize her words.

Standing at the sink, Tracy stared blankly out the kitchen window to her mother's flower garden. The weeds needed pulling, she could see that. That was something she could do and do well. Hurriedly, she rinsed the dishes and loaded the dishwasher. Then, forgetting she was fresh from the shower, she dashed to the back door, grabbing her mother's work gloves from their hook and heading for the flower garden.

Fifteen

Tracy took a deep breath and tried to prepare herself to face Beth and her family. Maybe her father's prayers would be answered today, for she knew he had prayed to have their family happily united, without the anger and undertow of resentment.

As he turned into the driveway of the two-story frame house, Tracy took another deep breath. Beth had a nice home, two remarkable children, a great husband. She must behave as though she were happy for her, not resentful.

As soon as the car stopped, the front door flew open and two children raced out to meet them. Tracy felt a sudden surge of tenderness for Chad, eight, and Amy, six. Both were blonde, like Ken, with Beth's soft brown eyes. They were dressed in cute playclothes, their faces scrubbed, every hair in place.

"Hi, you guys." Tracy got out, extending her arms. They ran to her, hugging hard, and she needed that. How on earth could she feel anything but overwhelming love for these two?

Ken rounded a corner of the house, wearing a chef's apron over jeans and a golf shirt. He was a handsome man of thirty-five, tall and slim, a boyish face beneath close-cropped hair. His gray eyes were keen, indicative of his intelligence. He was in the computer business and doing very well.

"Tracy! Welcome home," he said, hugging her lightly.

"Thanks, Ken. Good to see you." Her eyes lingered on his face for another few seconds, expecting to see something she could tag as phony, but then she realized he was genuine in his welcome. And she felt ashamed of herself for doubting him.

"Beth's in the kitchen fussing over the potatoes," he said, looking down at Tracy. "She already burned the pie."

"Beth burned the pie?" she asked, showing her dismay.

"Third time she's burned something this week," he said, good-naturedly. "She's excited that you were coming home."

"Aunt Tracy!" Amy pulled at her arm. "Will you come upstairs and see my dollhouse?"

"I want to show her my bike," Chad pouted.

"Okay, you two, I'll see the dollhouse and the bike. There's plenty of time. But first I want to say hello to your mother."

Her father had started talking to Ken as they walked back to the barbecue grill, and now Amy and Chad chased after their golden retriever, who had latched on to someone's shoe.

Tracy hurried up the walk to the front door, feeling anxious about seeing her sister again. So Beth wasn't so perfect after all, burning food all week. A wry little grin tilted Tracy's mouth as she opened the door and stepped into the foyer.

"Beth?" she called.

The living room to the right of the foyer was clean and neat, but the stairs were half-strewn with the children's toys. As she passed the den on her way to the kitchen, she saw a puzzle, half finished, scattered over the carpet, and a rip in a throw pillow. Her smile widened.

Following the scent trail of something burned, she ended up in the kitchen where Beth was bent down, peering through the glass of the oven door. She whirled, glancing over her shoulder.

"Tracy! Come over here and let me give you a hug. I don't dare take my eyes off the bread."

As Tracy closed the distance between them, she could see that Beth was thinner, and there was a pinched look around her eyes. She remembered how dependent Beth had always been on their mother, and suddenly all the hurt feelings vanished. It was clear that Beth, too, had suffered, and Tracy suddenly wanted more than anything for everyone to stop hurting, to be happy again.

She put her arms around Beth and hugged her hard. Suddenly they were both crying, and Beth was gasping out an apology. "So sorry... didn't mean what I said to you...."

Tracy was sobbing as well. "And I'm sorry for not being there. I am so very sorry...."

The kids were scrambling through the back door, bounding into the kitchen. The sisters pulled back, each wiping their eyes, while Amy and Chad came to a screeching halt, their little faces a study in concern as they looked from their aunt to their mother.

"Just tears of joy, kids," Beth sniffed. "I'm happy to see my little sister."

Tracy swallowed hard, hugging Beth again. It was going to be okay now. She felt a peace settling over her heart; the tears that had washed over her face seemed to have cleansed her soul as well.

It had been a good day for everyone, and as Tracy drove back home with her father, they sang in harmony to a favorite hymn, one they often sang in church.

"Dad," Tracy said, when their song had ended, "I'm coming to church with you in the morning."

He glanced across at her, his eyes reflecting an expression of joy. "I'll be very pleased for you to do that. And I promise not to preach past twelve!"

She rushed to her room to dress for the barbecue at Tommy Woodfin's house. Checking the clock, she saw that she barely had enough time to freshen up and change her clothes before Jay arrived.

She had decided to wear a denim sundress with red sandals and purse. Fluffing her hair, then redoing her makeup, she managed to be ready when Jay rang the doorbell at five-thirty.

"Hi," he said, looking relaxed in tan khakis and a white polo. "Ready to go?"

"I'm ready. Be home later, Dad," she called over her shoulder.

As they walked out to Jay's car, his fingers slipped through hers, and he grinned down at her. "It feels good to think about a fun evening. I'm working too hard."

"So am I. In fact, I promise not to mention work—" she winked—"after you give me the latest on the DeRidder case."

He groaned. "I should have known you'd ask. There is no *latest*. The man who picked up the ransom money is still in jail. I called headquarters today. They're still questioning him, but he swears he knows nothing about Jackie, that he was only trying to make some quick money to get out of Georgia."

Tracy frowned as she slipped into the front seat of his car. "So what's next?"

He shook his head. "I'm not sure. Guess I'll find out when I go back to Atlanta tomorrow."

Tracy kept her promise and said nothing more as they drove out of town, past Smoky's barbecue, getting a whiff of the hickory smoke floating in the air.

"Did your dad enjoy his meal last night?"

Tracy laughed. "Dad *always* enjoys his meal."

Jay made a right turn onto a road that climbed a beautiful hardwood ridge and led through a private gate, left open for guests. About two hundred yards past the gate, the road slowly veered left and gradually wound its way downhill and out of the dense forest.

Winding to the right, the road dropped over the last low hill and into a beautiful open valley with a long, narrow lake. The lake was shaped like an *L,* and Tracy could see Tommy's house nestled in the inside corner of the lake. Twelve to fifteen cars and pickups were parked in front of the house and halfway up the road.

"Tommy calls this house his 'camp' house, but it's much nicer than any camp house I've seen," Jay said with a wry grin.

"I agree." Tracy studied the two-story red cedar house with its weathered gray cedar-shake roof. The driveway held a variety of cars and pickup trucks, and as Jay parked, Tracy could hear loud voices and laughter from the rear of the house.

She smiled at Jay. "Sounds like a party."

As they got out of the car, a voice yelled, "It's Jay Calloway. Hide the booze, here comes the law!"

A roar of laughter broke out but Jay merely shook his head good-naturedly. "What a crew. Think you'll be able to put up with this rowdy bunch tonight?"

"Oh, I think so. You know, Jay, you and I aren't so different, after all. People always treated me a bit different because I was a preacher's kid, and they seem to put you on some kind of pedestal, as well."

Jay nodded thoughtfully. "You're right. I hadn't thought of it that way, but I now have a better understanding of how your life was when you were growing up."

As they walked toward the house, Tracy tried to recall the football players on Jay's team his senior year. They had made All-State and achieved lots of recognition.

He took her arm as they crossed the well-kept yard to the front of the house, but then Jay steered her around to the side.

"Sounds like the party's out back on the patio."

Tracy felt the old pang of nervousness that always assaulted her upon entering a crowd. She had been told it didn't make sense—Tracy Kosell the reporter who covered all kinds of stories but got stage fright over one small group.

As greetings were made and hands were shaken, she recalled most of the people. There were Jim and Fran Edwards, married right out of high school. Jim now had a spare tire around his middle but still had the sense of humor that had always gotten him in trouble. She realized it was his voice who had yelled, "Hide the booze, here comes the law."

Trey Wright, unmarried, was with a pretty girl whom Tracy judged to be about her own age. She, too, seemed rather bewildered by the rowdy group. The Albrecht twins—Jason and John—were there with their wives, whom Tracy did not know. They were friendly and greeted her warmly as she was introduced. She recognized half a dozen more who hovered about the grill, helping with the steaks. In all there looked to be about fifteen people. A couple of the guys appeared to be dateless, like Tommy, who was working hard at the grill. Everyone wore jeans or shorts and tennis shoes except Tracy, and she immediately felt overdressed in her sundress and sandals.

"Let's say hello to Tommy," Jay whispered to her, after he had made the introductions and steered her around the talkative crowd.

"Hey, man," Tommy called, glancing back over his shoulder.

"Hi, Tommy. You remember Tracy Kosell?"

Tommy smiled his charming smile. He had been the biggest, most handsome guy in school, with the broad shoulders and physique that had made him Moonglow's outstanding linebacker. He was still handsome, but there was a weariness around his eyes now, and the square face held some extra weight.

"Hey, Tracy. Been a long time."

"I know. I like your place."

He turned back to a steak that needed attention. "Thanks. How do you two want your steaks? Hope you don't say rare because we're one step past that."

"Medium for me," Jay answered.

"Well done, please."

Tommy turned and crinkled his nose at Tracy. "Finicky, huh?" He glanced at Jay. "What do you do in your spare time? I never see you."

"I hang out at Lake Lanier some. When I come to Moonglow, it's just a quick visit to see my parents."

"Hey, what'll you two have to drink?" John, the rowdy twin, asked.

"Just a Coke for me," Tracy answered.

"Make that two," Jay answered.

"Hey, you're off duty, aren't you?" Tommy nudged him. "Don't you want a splash of Jack Daniels?"

"No, thanks."

Tracy's eyes roamed the crowd where mixed drinks and beer were being passed out liberally, although there were some soft drinks visible as well.

She had always connected the fact that she was a preacher's daughter to her distaste for beer, thinking it was the foulest stuff she had ever been tempted to sip. One time only.

The conversation turned to past football games. Tommy reminded Jay of their last game together, when Jay had dropped an important pass, then redeemed himself by making the winning touchdown. Other guys started to mention key plays that won or lost a game, and Tracy began to wonder just how much she was going to enjoy the party since she didn't remember most of the games mentioned. Then the quiet girl with Trey walked over to her and struck up a conversation. She was drinking iced tea.

"I'm Elizabeth." She repeated her name for Tracy. "I know it's hard to grasp so many new names and faces at once."

Tracy laughed. "Thanks for being perceptive. I'm Tracy. Do you live in Moonglow?"

"No, I'm from Highlands." She was an attractive blonde, tall and slim.

"Oh." Tracy nodded, as her eyes slipped over to Jason, who brought a large platter from the house, heading toward the grill.

"How do you like Highlands?" Tracy asked. "Has it grown a lot over the past five years? That's how long it's been since I was up there."

"Yes, it grows more every year with all the development. We get a lot of Atlanta residents who want a weekend place in the mountains. I'm a realtor there," she explained with a smile.

"I see." Tracy nodded. "I'll bet the real estate prices have really soared."

Elizabeth smiled. "It's amazing what people are willing to pay for a small piece of undeveloped land. But I love it there. When I get bored, all I have to do is make a trip down to Atlanta and get wound up in the traffic and decide—hey, I don't need this. Where do you live, Tracy?"

"Los Angeles," Tracy replied, "and I know something about interstates, believe me."

"I'll bet. Think you'll stay there?"

"I'm not sure. To be honest, I miss the people here, although I don't see myself coming back to Moonglow."

Elizabeth had just asked a question about Los Angeles when Tommy called, "Come and get it!"

A roar of approval burst over the crowd as everyone turned to follow Tommy. He was hoisting a huge tray of steaks, followed by a procession of hungry-looking men. He led the way across the concrete patio and through the open glass doors into the basement. A long room that served as a den had been converted into a party room. Overstuffed sofas and chairs, bean-bags, lots of heavy lamps, and tables filled up the big room. Fish were mounted on the walls, along with a couple of deer antlers. A long bar crossed the far end, and behind the bar she could see a sink, refrigerator, and microwave.

Across the bar, the food was set up buffet style, with huge mounds of potato salad, baked beans, and several salads. At the end of the counter huge tumblers were lined up beside pitchers of tea. An ice bucket overflowed with ice, and on the floor an ice chest held more soft drinks and beer.

Sturdy gold paper plates and matching drink cups were stacked beside black napkins, carrying out the school colors. Tommy had obviously put a lot of thought into his party. Gold plastic forks were laid out beside wicked-looking steak knives. Tommy meant for everyone to enjoy their steak. Tracy's eyes widened as he handed out the special cooked orders, getting every one of them straight.

"Tracy, I hope this one suits you." He dug down into the platter and came up with a well-done steak.

"Who else is sharing this one with me?" she asked, amazed at the size.

"You look as though you live on breadsticks," Tommy teased as his eyes swept her slim frame.

"She probably does," Jay spoke up over her shoulder.

Tracy shrugged and laughed good-naturedly. There was no point in mentioning her metabolism. Let them think she fretted over her diet like many other women when, in truth, she never gave it a thought.

Everyone filled their plates and settled about the room, some at the eating bar, others at the card tables. Tracy followed Jay over to a huge leather sofa and coffee table, covered with a party cloth.

Taking a seat beside Jay on the sofa, Tracy glanced around

the pine-paneled walls, a perfect background for all the memorabilia displayed there. Football pictures in black frames boasted the teams from junior high through high school. Other pictures featured Tommy as captain, Tommy making tackles, Tommy accepting a trophy. One of the pictures featured Jay catching a long pass, and Tracy turned back to Jay, whose attention was centered on his food.

"Hey, you were quite a star." She nudged him.

"It was just a game." He glanced at the wall of pictures.

As Tracy's eyes passed over the room, seeing other mementos, it occurred to her there was nothing here to indicate Tommy's marriage to Lisa. She remembered that Lisa, a tall brunette with a wide smile, had been from Asheville. Tracy had only met her once, but she had thought she was very striking.

The chatter died down as everyone attacked their food. "Hey, Jay," one of the guys called across the room, "how's the investigation going?"

"On Jackie, you mean?"

Automatically, Tracy glanced at Tommy. He and Jackie had been inseparable in high school. Tommy was cutting his steak, but at the question, his movements slowed and a frown furrowed his brow. Tracy felt sorry for him. It must be awful to have cared a lot about someone who went off, married a rich guy, then simply disappeared.

"We made an arrest—a guy from Clayton."

Several voices chimed in at once with the same questions repeated almost in unison.

"Who is the guy?"

"And where is Jackie?"

Jay put up his hand to silence the onslaught of voices. "We haven't located her yet but hope to learn something soon."

Tracy noticed Jay didn't bother to elaborate, specifically on his doubts about the guy being the real kidnapper.

Tracy glanced back at Tommy, expecting him to ask something about the guy who had been arrested. He asked nothing. He continued to work on his steak in silence. *Different people show pain in different ways,* she thought. She imagined Tommy, always so strong and tough, had bottled up his feelings where Jackie was concerned.

"Jay, I heard you were one of the detectives who broke that gruesome murder last month," one of the guys spoke up. "The man who killed his wife and her lover."

"Could we talk about something else?" One of the women made a face. "My steak isn't looking so good."

"Right." Tommy glanced around at the group. "I've invested too much in these steaks not to have them appreciated. Besides, I want everyone to finish up in time to do some fishing. I've restocked the lake."

This comment brought on various responses of approval, and everyone dug heartily into their food, leaving off the chitchat.

When most of the plates were empty and tossed in a garbage can, some of the women went to freshen up. There was a bath downstairs and another one on the upper floor. Tracy chose the one in the hall on the second floor. It was masculine, done in brown plaids. Returning to the stairs, she passed an open door to a comfortable-looking living room with glass doors leading out onto an upper patio. She could see lawn chairs and an umbrella table there.

Back downstairs, Jay was waiting for her. "Ready to go fishing?"

"Didn't bring a rod." She smiled.

"Neither did I. I should have thought of it, but Tommy didn't mention fishing. I'm sure he's got some spares. Or we can just take a walk, if you like."

"A walk sounds good to me."

As they stepped out into the soft, humid evening, Tracy looked around the peaceful setting. The lake was about twenty yards from the house, approached by a wide, graveled path that led past the back side of the garage and barbecue area down to half a dozen lawn chairs beside the lakeshore and a thick willow. A couple of boats were tied up at the boat landing.

"Let's go this way." Jay took her hand as they walked away from the crowd toward a picnic bench set up on the far side of the lake.

"Tommy has done well with his construction company, hasn't he?" Tracy asked.

"Yeah. I think he's had to go in debt to acquire all he has, but from what I hear, business is booming."

As the voices of people having fun melted into the background, Tracy glanced up at Jay, feeling contented just to be with him.

"Thank you for inviting me," she said.

"I figured we both needed something like this. I have an idea that you work as hard as I do."

"Don't know if it's *as* hard, but I do work hard. Seems like I must thrive on it. I'm always looking for the next story."

As they approached the picnic table and took a seat, the lake spread before them like a gray satin cloth, the smoothness split here and there by the length of a fishing line. Down on the far end, one of the twins had just landed a big catfish.

"You like being near the water, don't you?" she asked Jay.

"I do. To me, it's very relaxing. In fact, if I couldn't go out to Lake Lanier every now and then and kick back, I'd probably have ulcers."

She laughed. "Do you rent a cabin there?"

"A guy I work with owns a little cabin and is nice enough to share it with some of the guys on the force. In return, we kick in at Christmas time and buy him something nice. Last year we bought a new refrigerator. This year we're planning to go out and build a little deck off the back of the cabin for him."

"That's really sweet," Tracy said. As her eyes traced his profile, it again struck her how much he appealed to her.

"You two having fun?" Tommy yelled. He had come halfway around the lake to bring a couple of fishing poles to Elizabeth and Trey.

"Yep, this is our idea of fun," Trey replied.

Tommy laughed. He passed out the poles and turned to head toward Tracy and Jay. In T-shirt and jeans, Tommy's body looked muscled and tanned from the time he spent in the sun. His hair grew thick and dark, down to his collar. He had more facial wrinkles than Jay, Tracy noted.

"Why didn't you bring a beer or something over here?" he asked Jay, then looked at Tracy. "I forgot. Preacher's daughter, right?"

Tracy nodded. "But that doesn't make me a prude. Besides, I couldn't put a drop of anything else in my stomach. That was great food, Tommy."

"Thanks." White teeth flashed behind a quick smile that disappeared as he turned back to Jay. "So you think you got the guy who kidnapped her?"

It was automatically understood who the *her* was.

Jay frowned. "I'm not sure, Tommy. He's pretty dumb."

Tommy chewed his lip, staring at Jay for a minute. "How smart do you have to be to grab a car and do away with the woman in it?"

Tracy winced at the impersonal way he referred to Jackie. He seemed to be blanking out the fact that the "woman" had once been his sweetheart.

"Yeah, well, we'll see," Jay replied.

"So if you two are happy as lovebirds, I'll leave you be." Tommy turned to go.

"What's that noise I hear on the other side of the woods?" Jay asked.

Tommy turned back, glancing east. "I'm putting in some trout lakes for a man from Clayton. He wants a quiet little place to come fishing." He glanced at his Rolex. "One of my guys is working late." He turned to survey his guests. "Well, let me get back to the party."

As he walked off, Tracy stared after him, a bit troubled.

"He didn't seem as concerned about Jackie as I would have expected."

Jay sighed. "Tommy's the macho type. Doesn't want to show his emotions, so he goes in the other direction. I see that all the time." He looked back at her. "Let's talk about you. How did it go today visiting your sister?"

Tracy pressed her back against the picnic table and crossed her legs. "It went very well. Jay, I have a great family. I guess I'm your typical black sheep."

"Oh, I don't think so." He tilted his head, looking down at her with an expression of affection. "Every family has its problems. With ours, it's my older brother. He's separated from his wife, Elizabeth, and if there's a divorce, it's going to hurt Mom and Dad more than anything."

"Separated?" She made a quick mental trip back to the brother two years older than Jay. She didn't know Elizabeth, the woman he had married. "What's their problem? Or is it personal?"

Jay shook his head. "I'm not sure. Michael's giving his new detective agency about fifteen hours a day, I think. He needs to spend more time with little Katie, their daughter. And Elizabeth is set on restoring an antebellum house she inherited from her grandmother. She's a clinical psychologist and dreams of operating a business out of the old house. But Katie complains that it's haunted, and Michael says the place is too far from his work." He shook his head. "A lot of couples have trouble in their marriages, I guess. But I honestly don't think they want a divorce. I know they both feel strongly about keeping their marriage vows. I hope they work things out."

Tracy listened thoughtfully. "I'm glad they respect their vows that much. I know lots of couples in Los Angeles who seem to divorce without a second thought. If things don't work, they're awfully quick to head to divorce court nowadays."

"When I marry, I want it to be for keeps," Jay said. "That's part of my faith, I guess. When I make a vow before God and man, I expect to honor it. Really, I think Michael feels the same way. We were raised in a loving Christian home, and Mom always taught us a lot of Scripture." He smiled at Tracy. "I guess Mom's a pretty good teacher, because what she taught me really stuck."

Tracy considered his words, spoken in a slow, thoughtful manner. She couldn't help wondering what it would be like to be married to Jay. When she realized the direction her thoughts had taken, she glanced quickly toward the lake, afraid that Jay might see something in her eyes.

"Well, I don't want to seem antisocial," Jay said. "Want to walk back over and see who's caught the biggest fish?"

She grinned. "Yeah, why not?"

The evening passed pleasantly although Tracy and Jay were the first ones to leave. Jay kept apologizing to Tracy. "Sorry to be a party pooper, but Dad and I got up early and worked hard all day. I'd forgotten how many repairs were needed at my parents' house and grounds. I had promised to help Dad catch up."

"No apologies are needed," she laughed. "I forgot to check in with Sam, and I'll have to do that before it gets too late. He's a family man and goes to bed soon after he tucks his sons in."

As they said their good-byes to the people at the party, Tracy realized how much she had enjoyed herself.

"You two come back anytime," Tommy said, looking from Jay to Tracy. His eyes lingered on her face for a moment, then whipped back to Jay. "Better hold on to this one, Jay."

Jay's arm slipped around her waist. "Yeah, I'm trying."

As they walked back to the car, Tracy wondered if he was really trying to hold on to her, or if he was just being polite.

They rode back into Moonglow, listening to a love song on the tape deck, and Tracy found herself liking Jay more each time she was with him. *Where will this lead?* she wondered. He seemed thoughtful as well, so she didn't bother trying to carry on a conversation.

He pulled into her driveway, then turned toward her. He leaned close to kiss her good-night, and she responded, more than before, despite the fact that the porch light, as always, beamed down into their faces.

"Well—" Jay finally pulled back from her—"I have the uncomfortable feeling that Reverend Kosell may be peering out a window, so I'll walk you to the door."

"I never seem to get away from the 'preacher's daughter' image," she laughed.

"You shouldn't want to," he said, as they climbed the front porch steps. "You've turned into a fine woman, Tracy Kosell."

He lowered his head and kissed her again, softly, tenderly, then turned and hurried down the steps.

She waved to him and reached for the door. But she wasn't ready to go inside. Instead, she reached in and flipped off the porch light, then wandered over to sit in the swing. Somewhere in the neighborhood a dog was barking, but soon the barking died away, and there was no sound except for the chirping of crickets and a night bird calling to his mate.

Sixteen

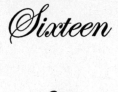

Somewhere in the distance a phone was ringing, and Tracy stirred in her bed, trying to think where she was. She heard footsteps approaching her room and she sat up, blinking sleepily and focusing on shapes outlined in the night light. She was back in Moonglow; this was her old bedroom.

"Tracy?" Her father stood in her doorway, wearing his bathrobe, the cellular phone in his hand. "There's a call for you."

"What?" She turned to look at the clock on her nightstand. It was 2:00 A.M. "What's going on, Dad?"

"I don't know. It's Jay." He handed her the phone and turned to leave the room.

"Hello?" She spoke quickly into the phone, still puzzled by the call.

"Tracy, this is Jay. Sorry to wake you and your father, but I thought you'd want to know. A pipe bomb went off about half an hour ago at the Olympic Village. At least a hundred people have been injured. I'm heading back to Atlanta now."

"What?" she gasped, bolting upright in bed. "Jay, that's incredible! I can't believe it. Do they know—"

"They don't know anything yet. There was a 911 warning that a bomb would go off in Centennial Park shortly before it happened. Look, I have to go. I debated on whether to call you or not, but—"

"I'm glad you did! I'll be back in the morning. And, Jay, be careful."

She hung up the phone and stared into space, trying to mentally absorb what she had just heard. "Dad?"

He stepped into her room. "What is it, Tracy? What's wrong?"

She grabbed a breath, then her words came in a rush. "Someone set off a pipe bomb at the Olympic Village about half an hour ago. Jay says over a hundred people are injured."

Her father sank into a chair by the dresser, visibly paling. "God, help them," he spoke softly.

"Oh, Dad. What's happening in this world? First, Flight 800 was blown up—"

"They haven't proved it was a bomb yet."

"But everything points to that so far. And now, with the millions of dollars spent on security for the Olympics, someone has managed to slip in a bomb." She shook her head, her eyes glazed with shock. "It's almost as if that bomb was a statement—'I can do whatever I want.'"

Richard sighed, leaning back in the chair. "Tracy, there's a lot of evil in the world. But what we must do is pray for God's protection, use some common sense, then go on with our lives. It's hard to make sense out of these things, I know that; and believe me, it's hard to give people answers. Very hard."

She smiled tenderly. "And everyone expects ministers to have all the answers. It isn't fair, is it, Dad?"

He shook his head and tried to smile. "It comes with the territory, honey." He pulled himself to his feet. "We'd better try and get some rest. I have a feeling I'll be getting lots of phone calls tomorrow."

"Good night," she said, slipping back down under the sheets. It was a long time since she had thought about all the demands made on her father, and yet he was so patient, so kind. Her mind drifted back over the years, to the hundreds of troubled people who had come to him for answers, for advice. He did his best to help.

She sighed, settling back on the pillow, as thoughts of the horrible incident in Atlanta filled her mind again. It was going to be a long night for many people.

"Oh, God, please, please help those who were injured. And bless and strengthen every person working to help."

She closed her eyes, thinking it was the first time she had offered an earnest prayer in quite a while.

Tracy was back in Atlanta by noon. She had left Moonglow shortly after eight, but traffic had been heavy on the interstate. It had taken her longer than usual to reach Buckhead. As she unlocked the door of her apartment, the telephone began to ring.

"This is Tracy," she answered hurriedly.

"Tracy, what's going on down there?" Sam sounded frantic. Glancing at the clock, she realized it was only nine o'clock in L.A. "I've been trying to reach you for two hours. Are you okay?"

Tracy sighed. "I'm fine, Sam, just upset by the bombing at Olympic Village."

"I've heard about the bomb. Give me the details."

"Here's what I know: Someone called 911 and warned that a bomb would go off. The caller was a white male with no distinct accent. The device was left near the sound and light tower during a concert. I'll have to tell you more later, Sam."

"How many casualties?"

Tracy closed her eyes, recalling the news report she had listened to on the radio as she drove back to Atlanta. "Two people dead, a hundred and ten injured. It's terrible."

"Do you think there's any connection to the DeRidder kidnapping?"

"Honestly, I don't think so. As I told you the other day, the guy who's been arrested still claims to know nothing of her whereabouts. He swears his call was merely an attempt to make some quick money. I've met with one of the lead detectives in the case. He thinks the guy is telling the truth. Apparently, nobody feels this guy was smart enough to pull off this complicated a kidnapping."

"So where does that leave the investigation?"

Tracy shrugged. "Back to square one, I suppose."

She could hear Sam's deep sigh, one that seemed to reverberate all the way from the West Coast. "Tracy, you gotta stay on top of this thing."

"Believe me, I'm doing my best. I'm going back to the club today to nose around some more. After all, it was the last known place she was seen. She drove out of the parking lot and into oblivion."

"She never called home again?"

"Once on her cell phone to check for messages. The housekeeper said she sounded fine. Give me a few more days, Sam."

"Well, we could always reshape the story. Do one on the bombing instead."

Tracy winced. It made her sick at heart to think her job turned on other people's tragedies. "I don't think I want to do that," she said tightly. "You know how I feel about capitalizing on other—"

"I know, I know. But I need a story, Tracy, or my boss is gonna be—"

"I'll have a story, Sam," she interrupted, unable to keep the note of irritation from her voice. "Just give me another day or two. And thanks for calling, but I have to run."

She hung up before she lost her temper completely. Fuming, she turned to the kitchen, needing some herbal tea to calm her nerves.

Turning on the TV while the teakettle heated, she sat glued to the screen in horror as the newscast ran footage of ambulances leaving the scene of the bombing. The explosion had sent shrapnel, screws, and nails flying for one hundred yards. The scene made her sick at heart, and she hit the remote, turning off the TV. Her father had taught her to pray when life became overwhelming, and now she bowed her head for the second time in twenty-four hours, praying for those involved in the blast and for the safety of the nation, as well, in the face of all that was happening.

Later, Tracy drove back to the country club, craning her neck for the talkative valet. He was not working today; instead, another man took her car.

"I'm having a late lunch," she informed him, then hopped out. She stood for a moment, glancing around, trying to visualize Jackie leaving from this place. She was feeling good, the valet had said; Jackie had obviously tipped him generously.

Thoughtfully, she hurried up the steps and went back inside to study the layout of the club.

A hall led away from the main foyer, and she wandered toward the ladies' room, examining the luxurious interior. No doubt Jackie had come in here that day, since there was a separate powder area with comfortable seats before a huge gold mirror.

Tracy sat down on one of the seats, absently running her finger over the creamy beige, marble countertop. She imagined

Jackie touching up her hair, looking into the mirror, thinking of the gala evening being planned at the Olympics' opening ceremonies. She stared blankly at her own reflection, thinking of Jackie making plans to go home but first calling the housekeeper.

Calling the housekeeper.

Jay had told her they already obtained phone records; there were no calls made that couldn't be explained.

Tracy got up and wandered out, not sure which way her mind was moving or exactly what was motivating her, but she stopped at the pay phone just outside the ladies' lounge.

For a moment, she merely stared at it. Jay said Jackie had not called home on a private line here but rather on her cellular phone. She wouldn't have used this pay phone. Across the way she spotted the Oak Room. Jay had said she met a friend for lunch in the Oak Room. The friend had said there was nothing unusual about Jackie that day; everything seemed fine when the friend left to relieve the nanny.

Tracy walked to the door and peered inside. It was smaller than the other dining rooms, a cozy elegant area with linen tablecloths and pastel roses in crystal vases on each table. A nice place to sit and chat and look through the glass wall to the golf course. She decided to take her chances.

The staff was busy today since it was Saturday. A TV screen in a corner of the room revealed the pandemonium of the bombing that had taken place in the wee hours of the morning. There was a somber mood throughout the entire club, and in here, conversations were being carried on in low-modulated voices, almost as though everyone felt the need to speak confidentially.

A distracted-looking hostess came forward. Tracy was relieved to see this was not the same one who had brushed her off last week.

"I'm just waiting on a friend." She smiled.

"Would you like to have a seat at the bar?"

Tracy glanced toward the small bar tucked discreetly in a far corner. "Yes, maybe I will."

She wandered toward the bar, wondering why she hadn't noticed it last week when she peered in. Actually, she had never really looked around after being informed this was a members-only club.

Today everyone was distracted, and as she gazed across the room, she observed this dining room and bar catered more to women than men. The bar was a small semicircle, without the glass mirrors or the obvious display of bottles. Two women dressed in business suits sat midway along the bar, each sipping exotic-looking drinks.

A nice-looking woman in her early forties took a seat next to Tracy and called out to the young bartender efficiently serving a woman at the opposite end.

"Charlie, I need a quick fix."

"Be right there." The bartender gave her a charming smile.

The woman turned to Tracy. "Sorry. Am I jumping in ahead of you?"

"It's okay. I have plenty of time." Tracy tried to appear friendly, yet nonchalant. "Actually, I'm new here, so I'm just wandering around, getting acquainted with the facilities. Incidentally, my name is Tracy Kosell."

"Shirley Blakely—" the woman extended her hand—"I think you'll be pleased with the club. I'm in here three or four times a week. Service is excellent." Shirley glanced from Tracy back to the bartender.

The woman's designer suit and purse, Tracy decided, would exceed a month's paycheck from her reporting job. It was hard for her to imagine this kind of world.

"The usual?" The bartender had reached their side and was now giving the woman an obliging smile.

"A double. Got a rough one today, Charlie."

"Sorry to hear that, Mrs. Blakely." He glanced at Tracy, obviously not recognizing her as one of his regulars.

"I haven't decided what I want yet," Tracy informed him. "Go ahead and get hers while I think about it." Tracy spoke matter-of-factly, trying to sound like someone who knew her way around.

Tracy looked back at the woman, deciding to take a chance. "Do you know my friend Jackie DeRidder?"

The woman's head swiveled as she cocked an expertly waxed eyebrow. "Jackie? Sure. What's the latest on her?"

"There's still no trace of her. And the man they've arrested doesn't seem capable of masterminding a kidnapping. I'm really worried," Tracy said, shaking her head. This was the truth, and it was easy to convey her concern. She remembered the real Jackie, not the superficial person she seemed to have become.

"You know what?" The woman looked around, lowered her voice, then leaned closer. "I wonder if she didn't take off on her own."

Tracy tried to hide her dismay. "That's an idea," Tracy returned smoothly. "But I don't think Jackie would give up this lifestyle. You know how she liked the good life."

The woman shrugged. "Did you talk to her last week?"

Tracy cleared her throat. "Actually, I was in L.A. But I've known Jackie all her life, and I know she can be unpredictable."

Charlie delivered the drink, and the woman made a grab for it, taking a long, deep swallow.

"Decide yet?" Charlie turned to Tracy.

Now what? Tracy thought. She didn't drink, and she wasn't about to start now. "Tell you what. Just bring me a ginger ale with a twist of lime."

"Coming right up." He turned to go.

"Don't you want a splash of vodka in it?" her new friend asked discreetly. "No smell, you know. I've arranged a special meeting with my attorney this afternoon, and I need a smoother. I'm trying to get more money from my ex-husband."

"Oh." Tracy sighed. "Well, I don't really care for vodka."

The woman took another long sip, then returned her attention to Tracy. "So you've known Jackie all her life?" The woman tilted her head back, eyeing her thoughtfully beneath a double coat of mascara.

"Yes, and I'm worried about her, to be quite honest. I mean, her life has gotten rather complicated lately, you know."

"Boy, do I! What bothers me is, we sat here and got plastered together the day she disappeared."

Tracy caught her breath. "Were you the one she met for lunch?"

"No, that was Merilee Champion. Jackie and I hung out here for fifteen minutes or so before I had to get back to the office. She was feeling pretty good after that last double martini. I had to leave then. But she shouldn't have been driving," she said under her breath, taking another drink.

Tracy felt as though she were creeping around in a dark room, feeling for the right objects. She had to play this just right; the woman beside her was her best streak of luck so far.

"Her drinking was getting to be a problem, wasn't it?" Tracy remarked in a low voice. "Still, if there had been an accident, we would have heard right away."

The woman shrugged. "I know. That's been my consolation." She polished off her drink and sat it down with a thud. "Well, I'm outta here. Nice meeting you...er, what was the name?"

"Tracy. I'll see you again."

"Right."

She slipped from the bar stool and turned on her spike heel

to gracefully exit the room, every hair in her perfectly styled coiffure in place. From the corner of her eye, Tracy watched her go, wondering how much alcohol would hit her blood by the time she got behind the wheel of her car.

Charlie placed the ginger ale before her and hesitated. "Do you have a tab here?"

She reached into her purse, feeling no pressure to be overly nice. Silently, she handed him a ten-dollar bill.

"Thanks, I'll get your change."

As she considered her options, Tracy let her eyes roam over the crowded room. Mentally, she was assessing the information she had gleaned from her talkative friend. She doubted she'd get this lucky again—someone willing to talk to a stranger about Jackie—but she decided to try the bartender. "Do you know my friend Jackie DeRidder?" she asked casually, sipping her ginger ale.

The friendly look in his eyes turned to one of guarded reserve. "She was a member of the club. Are you?" he asked pointedly.

"No, I'm not," she returned frankly. "But I am a friend of Jackie's, and her family is very concerned. Did she use that phone before she left that day?" she asked, indicating the phone behind the bar.

He arched a brow and answered, rather formally, "No, she did not. Excuse me."

He turned to another customer, and Tracy knew she would get no further with him. It was just like last week; clearly everyone had been told not to discuss the DeRidders. She'd been lucky to corner the valet, but unfortunately he was not working today. Maybe tomorrow she'd try again.

She finished her drink and left the Oak Room, hesitating outside the door. Now what? Her eyes returned to the pay phone adjacent to the ladies' lounge.

Tracy frowned. Why had Jackie not used the phone in the Oak Room to call her housekeeper? She chewed her lip, thinking back to high school days when Jackie could be a bit sneaky about skipping classes to hang out with her friends at the café nearby. Jackie could be more than sneaky, she decided, measuring the climb she had made from a logger's shabby house in a rural area outside of Moonglow to Martin DeRidder's mansion in Buckhead. Maybe she made another call besides the one to her housekeeper, one she didn't want registered on her cellular phone. A long-distance call?

The tennis pro had an airtight alibi, Jay had said. Another suave businessman she had seen here at the club that day who lived outside of Atlanta? Or had she met up with someone here and arranged a little rendezvous later? And maybe something went wrong.

She stood before the pay phone, staring at it. Thoughtfully she touched the cord. Then she reached into her purse and pulled out her pen and notepad, jotting down the telephone number listed on the phone. It wouldn't hurt to check out the phone calls made from this phone; if Jackie were having a private conversation that she didn't want showing up on her phone records, she wouldn't use her cellular phone, and she couldn't talk privately in the Oak Room. It was a long shot, but long shots were better than no shots, and the case wasn't getting anywhere, except for the arrest of this guy who seemed to know nothing of Jackie's whereabouts.

She would ask Jay to trace the calls from this phone on the day Jackie disappeared. She could imagine him wincing, dismissing the idea as unworthy of the time taken to explore the possibility. But on this one, she was going to dig her heels in and insist on getting the calls traced on all the pay phones at the club. It was just a wild hunch, but it seemed to be as good as any other theory she had heard. And time was running out for Jackie, wherever she was.

Seventeen

Tracy was pleasantly surprised when Jay called shortly after six. "Hi, how are you?" he asked.

"I'm fine. So what's going on?"

He sighed. "Enough to warrant a good dinner break. I need a special evening—how about having dinner with me at Canoe?"

"At Canoe? I'd love it. Want me to meet you there?" she offered.

"Do you mind? I'm on a tight schedule. What about eight?"

"Perfect." She smiled to herself. "See you then."

She had never been to Canoe, but she'd heard it was one of the new glamour spots in Atlanta. Celebrities were often spotted there, and there was even a rumor that the president had been in. As she pulled into the parking lot, she glanced at the beautiful setting of the casually swank Canoe. Located along the Chattahoochee River, it was a relaxing place to come for dinner. Certainly others seemed to think so, for the parking lot was filled.

She hurried up to the door, where Jay was waiting just inside.

"Hi." He smiled at her as though glad to see her. "I have a table waiting."

"It certainly pays to know the VIPs in this town. Glad I know you," she said, nudging him teasingly.

"It's one of my favorite places." He took her by the elbow as the hostess led the way.

Tracy's eyes roamed over the brick walls, up to the arched ceiling, and back to Jay. The aroma of wonderful food filled the air. After they were seated in a booth, she leaned back and looked at Jay, suddenly realizing she was famished.

"I'm surprised you could take a dinner break," she said.

"I had to! I've been going on fast food and cold coffee or warm tea." He grinned across at her. "Besides, I'd much rather look at you than Bill."

She laughed. "I imagine he's pretty uptight."

"Who isn't?" Jay sighed, as menus were placed before them.

When their server returned, Jay chose quail, but Tracy had a yen for crab cakes. After their orders were taken and iced tea was placed before them, she decided to get right to the point.

"What's the latest on Jackie?"

The glow in his eyes dimmed. "I'm beginning to suspect your motive for being with me is to get information on the case."

Tracy bristled. Already they were in the reporter/detective conflict, and she knew she should smooth over her question, but she was in no mood.

"That's right, Jay," she returned sarcastically. "It's why we had so much fun at the barbecue last night. I peppered you with questions, remember? And then—"

"Okay." He put up a hand. "Sorry. Maybe having dinner with me wasn't a good idea. I'm really on edge." He leaned forward, lowering his voice. "Our only suspect clearly knows nothing of Jackie's whereabouts. So, we're back to square one.

The mayor is all over us, and Martin DeRidder is climbing the walls. Now we have this bombing in the midst of the Olympics." He shook his head. "I'm ready to quit this business, move to Lake Lanier, and sell fish bait."

She nodded, feeling sorry for him. "Well, here's something that might help your case. I had an interesting conversation at the club today concerning Jackie."

"The club meaning Jackie's club?"

"Right." She paused as their food was placed before them. After the server left, Tracy leaned over her plate, lowering her voice. "You may want to question a woman named Shirley Blakely, who was probably the last person to talk with Jackie before she vanished. I met her in the Oak Room at the club."

"You have my attention," he said, ignoring his food.

Carefully, she repeated her conversation with Shirley Blakely at the bar, emphasizing the fact that Jackie had been drinking, that her drinking companion felt she might have taken off on her own.

Jay stared at her. "Why would she do that?"

"I don't think she did. Jackie had climbed too many rungs on the ladder to get to the top; she wouldn't give it up. I think what she might do is leave the club for a quick rendezvous before going home to change clothes for the opening ceremonies. Maybe that's why she called home to see if there were any messages."

"Nope." He picked up his fork and speared into his salad. "We've questioned the housekeeper over and over. She was emphatic about there not being any messages for Jackie."

"That's not the point," she insisted. "If nothing was pressing, she had a little extra time. I'm thinking she called home to say she was running late."

He looked up, the expression in his eyes taking on a new light. "As a matter of fact, she did say that. But everyone assumed it was because the traffic was heavy. Or at least, that was Mr. DeRidder's opinion. Everyone in Atlanta is running late with so many people on the streets and interstates."

"But what if she left here and went some other place in Buckhead?"

He nodded. "Met someone, you mean. We checked out the tennis pro. He was giving lessons all afternoon."

Tracy began to eat, although she was scarcely tasting the delicious food. "Not him. She was probably bored with him already. No, I'm thinking there might have been someone else."

Jay looked up, curious. "Who?"

"Look, I know it's a wild card, but would you put a trace on the pay phones at the club?"

"Why? She called on her cellular. And it was the only call made."

"But she might not use her cellular on a call she didn't want traced. Jackie was sharp and a bit sneaky. She liked to put one over on people, remember? What if she did use the pay phone at the club before she left? She must have; otherwise, there would be a record of her call on the cellular phone."

He stared into space, saying nothing for a moment.

Tracy sighed. Why wasn't he excited about this news?

The sound of his beeper broke through their conversation, and he closed his eyes and heaved a sigh.

Checking the number, he looked around the restaurant. "Excuse me. I have to find a phone."

She nodded, hoping their evening wasn't about to end. She simply had to stop pelting him with questions. There was no way he could enjoy his meal with her constant referrals to the case that had become such a headache for everyone.

Glancing around at the diners, she noticed the somber faces, the gloomy mood that seemed to dominate the club. It was the horrible bombing that had taken place. She, too, was feeling a dreariness pulling at her, one she couldn't shake.

Jay returned to the table and took a seat, lifting his fork. "Just as I suspected. I'll have to leave as soon as I wolf down the rest of my dinner."

Looking at him, she sensed the kind of pressure he must be experiencing. So much seemed to be expected of the police department, the investigators, the FBI. And yet, with everyone working, so little progress seemed to be made with the DeRidder case and even the bombing.

"Anything you can talk about?" she asked gently.

He shook his head, touching his mouth with the napkin. "Nope, sorry. Look, I apologize. Guess this was a bad idea."

She reached across, touching his hand. "Jay, being with you is never a bad idea." She realized she meant those words as she spoke them, and a look of appreciation touched his face.

"Thanks, Tracy. And being with you is the highlight of my otherwise dreary day."

"Leave when you need to," she reassured him. "I'll be fine. I may even have one of these tempting desserts."

"Please do." He was removing his wallet, motioning to the server.

"I'm kidding about the dessert." She looked at him, wondering what sort of investigation he was on now. "Jay, be careful." His job could be a dangerous one, she knew that, and yet he seemed to take everything in stride.

"Thanks. I'll call you tonight if it isn't too late. Otherwise, first thing in the morning."

Watching him go, she was aware that other heads turned in his direction as well. He was a very handsome man, and she was getting spoiled by being with him. Life was going to be very different when she returned to L.A. She didn't even want to think about it.

Turning back to her tea, she trailed a finger absently around the rim of the glass, her thoughts focusing. Maybe she would ask Sam for another week....

Eighteen

%

Tracy shut off the alarm clock and snuggled deeper under the covers on Monday morning. She had stayed glued to the news reports all day Sunday, and though there were some leads on the bomber, there were still no breakthroughs. She hadn't heard from Jay all day, to her disappointment. But it was Sunday, after all. She just hoped she hadn't put him off Saturday night with her questions.

Now, though her mind coaxed her to drag out of bed and get her day started, her body rebelled. She had not slept well. She kept thinking of the poor people injured in the bombing, of Jay out trying to catch criminals, and of Jackie DeRidder. Where had she gone? What had happened to her? As her dad had said, how could a beautiful blonde in a black Mercedes vanish into thin air?

Tracy stared at the ceiling. Her eyes narrowed. She couldn't. Someone, somewhere, knew where she was. And if she was alive or dead.

That thought brought her out of bed, and she trudged to the kitchen. As she passed through the living room, her eyes lingered on the French doors leading out to the courtyard. It was such a pleasant experience living here, and even though she knew she couldn't afford to pay the rent for long, she was glad she had splurged.

In the kitchen, she put the kettle on, reached for her tea bags, and debated giving Sam a call at home. Better not. Even Sam didn't roll out of bed at six in the morning.

Sighing, she recalled the urgency in his voice and thought of how little she had accomplished on this story. She flipped on the radio in the kitchen and stood transfixed as an announcer related the morning news.

Some good leads had been reported on Sunday in the search for the Olympic bomber. Meanwhile, the Georgia National Guard had brought in more troops to safeguard against a repeat attack. There had been no other devices discovered by late yesterday, and today was the busiest day yet for the summer games. The U.S. baseball team would be playing Cuba, the track-and-field events were filled, and eighty-six women would be competing in the women's marathon.

Patient crowds, undergoing heavier security checks, seemed determined to enjoy the Olympics. The Olympic Village was scheduled to reopen tomorrow.

The kettle began to sing, and she dropped a tea bag in her cup and poured the steaming water over it. Reaching into the cabinet, she removed a toaster pastry and popped it into the toaster. Her only rationalization that she was eating a nutritious breakfast was the "low fat" claim on the package.

She had made numerous calls to her Associated Press contacts here, and nobody seemed to know anything more than she did concerning the DeRidder case.

A plan began to form in her mind as she sat down to eat breakfast. She was going back to Martin DeRidder's house. She would drive up to the door and try to get an interview with someone. Anyone. And in the meantime, she would even call his office, try to get some news from someone there. After all, she was a friend of Jackie's.

Her hopes were short-lived when finally she reached Mr. DeRidder's assistant and was told he was out of the office. Furthermore, there was "absolutely no comment" on personal matters.

"But I'm a friend of Jackie's, and—"

"Excuse me, I don't mean to be rude. But I have nothing more to say," the woman informed her briskly.

The phone clicked in Tracy's ear. Sighing, she hung up and returned to her tea and her muddled thoughts. She felt like a monster intruding on other people's privacy; there had to be another way to get a lead in Jackie's disappearance.

Then suddenly she remembered something. She had gone home to interview some of Jackie's relatives, then gotten side-tracked when Jay told her someone had been arrested. The tragedy at Olympic Village had brought her back to Atlanta on Saturday, and she still had not done any of those interviews.

Today was Monday. She'd see what she could turn up in Atlanta. If there was nothing, she would return to Moonglow and interview some members of Jackie's family. Perhaps she would have to put her alternate plan into action: write about the poor little country girl who had gone to town, married one of the wealthiest men in the nation, then vanished into thin air.

She nodded thoughtfully, thinking this was the right decision. With her enthusiasm mounting again, she finished off her breakfast and rushed upstairs to dress.

The DeRidder mansion was even more imposing on this cloudy morning. Across the sprawling grounds and at the iron gate, security had been tripled, if that were possible. Cars jammed the circled driveway behind the gates, and bodyguards swarmed like flies. Of course, nobody could be sure the bombing and kidnapping were not linked in some way, since DeRidder's company had been a major benefactor to the Olympics. Still, she had a feeling there was no connection. Particularly after her chat with the woman at the club.

She drove on around the block to another section of homes, parked out in front of a wall, and reached for her tennis shoes. She was wearing shorts, T-shirt, and baseball cap. The perfect uniform of the serious jogger.

Tucking her purse under the seat of her car, she grabbed her car keys and got out, locking the door and placing her keys in the pocket of her shorts.

She leaned against the car for a moment, stretching each leg, rolling her neck, then doing some exercises designed to loosen up. She hadn't jogged in weeks, but if she were going to get back in the habit, she couldn't have selected a safer neighborhood.

She began at a slow pace, then picked it up as she turned the corner of the block. She passed a guy walking his dog, who gave her a friendly greeting, then pressed on. Up ahead she could see the brick walls surrounding the DeRidder mansion. Her steps slowed, and now she was just a lazy jogger as she tried to take in every detail of the manicured lawn, the imposing brick house, the assortment of cars parked in the driveway. When she came even with the gate, she leaned down, retying both shoelaces. Just as she did, a white Mercedes roared out of the drive. She looked into the face of an older, distinguished-looking man with silver hair and the kind of tan one acquires in expensive resorts. His eyes met hers momentarily, then he pulled smoothly into the street and drove off.

She stood staring after the car. She had seen enough newspaper clippings to know this was Martin DeRidder. Jackie had married this man? She shook her head, resuming her jogging.

Well, she had accomplished one thing. She had looked into Martin DeRidder's face, and she was not so sure he wasn't capable of revenge on an unfaithful wife.

Once she returned to her car, unlocked the door, and hopped inside, she decided to drive around Buckhead for a while. She stopped at several shops and a few eateries but got nowhere in pinpointing information about Jackie.

When she returned home that afternoon, her message light was blinking. She trudged toward the phone to obtain the message, certain it was Sam hounding her again. To her surprise, it was Jay, asking her to call his pager number immediately.

Eagerly, she sat down at the desk phone and dialed the number. She hung up and waited, hoping for good news this time. Maybe there had been an amazing stroke of luck and Jackie had been found. Or she had returned home. She switched on the TV to CNN, but there was nothing about Jackie, only more on the bombing.

Jay sat in his office, his feet swung up on his desk, his hands steepled before him as he leaned back in his chair and considered his progress on the DeRidder case. Tracy had been more help than he had admitted. Maybe it was time to thank her. He hoped she'd call back soon.

His pager beeped. He checked the number and smiled as he dialed Tracy's number.

"Hi, Tracy, it's Jay. Well, I owe you one."

"Oh, how's that?" she asked.

"At 12:35 on Friday, Jackie called her housekeeper on her cellular phone to check messages and to say she was running late. That was the only call she made. But guess what? We checked out the calls on the pay phones at the club. On the one near the Oak Room, there was a call made at 12:30. Guess where?"

"I have no idea, so *please* don't keep me in suspense," she responded, sounding breathless.

"Woodfin Construction in Moonglow. Tommy Woodfin's company." He reached for the notes on his desk, again going over his hurried handwriting, a slanted style that often only he could translate.

She gasped into the phone. "Have you called Tommy?"

"Nope. I'm going to Moonglow first thing in the morning to check it out. You remember Smoky saw a blonde driving a black Mercedes? And Smoky's place is on the way to Tommy's farm."

"Of course! And, Jay, I thought Tommy reacted strangely at the barbecue when we talked about Jackie's disappearance."

Jay frowned, lifting his eyes from his notes to stare into space, recalling that afternoon. "You're right," he agreed, marveling again at her perceptivity. "But that doesn't mean he had anything to do with it. Still, I'd be very interested in knowing what she said to him. If, in fact, she called him...."

"I think she did! And if there was something going on, don't you think Mr. DeRidder is capable of jealousy, a jealousy that could overpower his common sense and good nature? Don't you think an irate husband could be pushed into doing something rash?"

Jay ran that scenario through his mind once more. "Of course I think that. The husband is always investigated. However, Mr. DeRidder was at his office most of the afternoon. We can account for his whereabouts with the exception of half an hour."

"A lot can happen in a half hour," Tracy answered quickly. "He could have a discreet meeting with...." Her voice trailed off.

"With whom?" Jay prompted, staring at the mound of papers on his desk. "I can tell something is perking in your brain."

"Well, people do hire people to do unsavory jobs."

"A hit man?" Jay hiked an eyebrow. "Come on, Tracy. That just doesn't fit DeRidder's profile. This man is one of the most highly respected men in Atlanta. And remember, he adored her. He's sick with worry."

"Or regret. Okay, sorry for casting aspersions. Still, as a detective, you no doubt consider all angles."

"Considering them is one thing. Speaking publicly about them is another matter," he spoke softly into the phone. He didn't want to think about the implications of an overt investigation of Martin DeRidder. Still, he was a good detective, and he had never shied away from exploring all angles. He couldn't afford to do that now.

"I think I get your point," Tracy replied, and he heard the sigh in her voice. He wondered if she was thinking he was afraid of DeRidder.

"You know—" he hesitated for a moment, flipping through some of his notes—"I'm beginning to think you've missed your calling. You should be a detective rather than a reporter."

She laughed. "No, thanks."

"Look, I want to talk to Tommy face-to-face, gauge his reaction on whether Jackie did or didn't call him. Maybe the way he reacted on Saturday seemed out of character because she told him something he didn't repeat to us. And there's a possibility that the call to his company is merely a coincidence. After all, he does have a thriving business."

"In Moonglow. But not here. Jay, it means something; I know it does. I think she had a few drinks, acted impulsively—which was typical of the Jackie I remember—and she took off to Moonglow."

He rubbed his brow, trying to ease the tension headache that had been nagging him all day. "That's the part that isn't feasible, Tracy. She knew she had to meet her husband at four."

"Yeah, but we're talking interstate all the way, and by pushing it—"

"Even by pushing it," Jay interrupted, "she couldn't get to Moonglow and back in time."

"Jay, maybe Tommy came down here. Maybe we're letting Smoky's comments distract us."

"Well, we'll find out. Look, I'm going to be tied up this evening on a murder in Marietta. But by tomorrow afternoon—"

"Tomorrow I'll see you in Moonglow. I'll be at Dad's house."

He chuckled. "You are one determined lady! I'll call when I get there."

"Thanks a lot. And Jay...be careful."

He nodded, appreciating her warning. "Thanks, Tracy." He hung up the phone, staring at it for a moment. Then he shook his head, as if clearing it from thoughts too troubling to focus on.

After she hung up the phone, Tracy realized that Jay had gone out on a limb, telling her about the call on the pay phone. Remembering their previous arguments, she was surprised he was so free with the information, but then Jay was looking at her differently. Was he feeling about her as she was about him? Could she hope he was falling in love with her? Like it or not, she was falling in love with Jay Calloway. She smiled to herself, staring into space. What was wrong with that? He was a wonderful guy.

"I'll tell you what is wrong," she said into the silence of the room. "Location and career." She had to face the gloomy facts. Jay Calloway was a closemouthed detective in Georgia; she was a tough reporter in L.A. Their relationship didn't have a chance.

The thought depressed her. To distract herself, she pushed her mind toward clothes. Laundry. She had to do laundry. She hurried to the bedroom to gather up some items to throw in the washer. She would be leaving Atlanta first thing in the morning. She needed to be ready.

Nineteen

◊

Bright and early Tuesday morning, Tracy called the office and left a message for Sam, who was out. Then she locked up and headed for Moonglow. Once she hit I-85, she pressed her sandaled foot hard against the accelerator and checked the sides of the road for highway patrolmen. How fast could someone make it to Moonglow, given the extra Olympic traffic?

An hour and twenty minutes later, she turned off the highway leading down the old road to Moonglow. Looking to the northeast, she could see Rabun Bald, standing like a sentinel 4,700 feet tall, over the valley and coves.

The special cove where Jackie had lived was Tracy's first destination, and with that in mind she drove on through Moonglow and headed north. She rattled over the bridge of a small creek that wound its way deep into the mountains. As she drove along, trying to remember which dirt road to take, she came to a country store.

She had never been to Jackie's old home place, but Jay had given her directions for finding it. She remembered that this was where she was instructed to turn, and she made a sharp left up the hollow that wound from the valley floor past a small farm. Some of the roads here seemed to just disappear from the valley into the coves. The early pioneers had homesteaded this area, and ever since that time, many of the descendants continued to live along the coves and hollows.

Approaching a narrow, rutted road, the third one to her left, she made another sharp turn that appeared to lead to the back side of nowhere.

As Tracy swung the wheel to miss a pothole, she thought of Tommy Woodfin. He had traveled this road many times to pick up Jackie for dates during their high school years; it hadn't mattered to him that her family was poverty-stricken, even though he came from an upper-middle-class family. How had his parents felt about Jackie? Tracy couldn't remember.

She conceded that she and Jay could be chasing a total coincidence on the call from the pay phone. Her instincts argued back with her; she kept remembering the strange look on Tommy's face when Jackie's name was mentioned.

Another image floated into her mind's eye—Tommy packing Jackie's schoolbooks under his arm between classes; the adoring eyes she had cast upward to his handsome face. They had made quite a couple. Tommy was the star football player; she was the class beauty. Tracy remembered how she had envied Jackie's long legs and striking figure.

She sighed. She didn't envy her now. Dad was right. All the money she could want obviously had not brought her happiness. It was quite possible she had been seeing Tommy.

Thoughts of a jealous husband kept circling around in Tracy's brain. Martin DeRidder had been so generous, so loving. He would be brokenhearted to know she was having an affair behind his back. The man had a sterling reputation, according to Jay, and had contributed huge sums of money to worthy causes. Still, he was a man, a human being capable of normal emotions. How far would jealousy or anger push him?

Another curve and the road came to a dead end before the driveway of a small, run-down frame house. From the description she had been given, this had to be the house where Jackie had been raised. Her parents had been killed in a car accident shortly after Jackie graduated from high school. There had been no reason for her to come home afterwards. An older brother had moved to Detroit, Jay had said. But who lived here now?

The yard was overgrown with weeds and strewn with battered toys. She climbed the cracked concrete steps to the front porch and sidestepped a buckled plank to knock on the door.

She could hear a child crying somewhere in the house as a strange, yet vaguely familiar, aroma drifted through an open window.

Tracy twitched her nose, trying to think what that aroma was, just as a haggard-looking woman in her thirties jerked the door open.

Her hair hung straight and limp to her shoulders; her eyes were weary and unfriendly, and her jeans and T-shirt had been soiled by the whimpering baby boy in diapers, balanced on her hip.

"Hi," Tracy smiled. "Sorry to bother you, but—"

"If you're selling something, we can't buy it." She started to slam the door.

"Actually, I'm buying." The words burst from Tracy's mouth and she bit her lip, wishing some of the things that jumped from her head to her mouth could pass through an area of common sense.

Still, she had the woman's attention. The door opened wider.

"What are you buying?" She eyed Tracy suspiciously.

"Well," Tracy swallowed, "I'm Tracy Kosell. I was raised here and then went away to L.A."

The woman fidgeted, her eyes darting over Tracy, willing her to get to the point.

"I work for Associated Press, and I'm doing a story on Jackie DeRidder."

The woman groaned and began to shake her head. "Look, Wally's getting pretty mad about people coming up here, poking their nose in our business. Just because she's his cousin—"

"Wally is Jackie's cousin?" She racked her brain, trying to remember a Wally who had been in school with them, but nobody came to mind. She didn't recall Jackie having any relatives in high school when she knew her.

"We already told what we know. Which ain't nothing. Jackie had nothing to do with her relatives once she got highfalutin in Atlanta. Didn't want to claim kin, even. Besides, I thought they got the man who kidnapped her."

Tracy made a quick mental journey over her options. She decided to be honest. "I don't think the guy knows where she is. He was only trying to take advantage of the situation and get the ransom money."

The woman bit her lip, looking confused. "Didn't know that."

"May I leave a phone number with you? If you wouldn't mind asking your husband to call me tonight, I'd really appreciate it. I'm Reverend Kosell's daughter, and I'll be at his house."

Tracy had dug a pad and pen from her handbag and was jotting down the number as the baby started to flail his arms and cry in earnest. She handed the paper to the woman, who was bouncing the little boy on her hip.

"What kind of story are you writing?" the woman asked, studying Tracy's hairdo.

"Just a story about Jackie. How she went from Moonglow to Buckhead in Atlanta, then disappeared. But apparently," she added deliberately, "her husband's money didn't make her happy."

"Nah, she wasn't happy." Her eyes darted away from Tracy

after she spoke those words, and she stepped farther back into the living room. "My cabbage is burning."

The door slammed in Tracy's face, and she stood for a moment, staring at the rough frame exterior badly in need of paint. How did this woman know Jackie wasn't happy? Had Wally talked to Jackie?

Pondering that thought, she headed back to the car. A light rain was starting to fall, adding to the bleak gray of the house and yard. Tracy tried and failed to imagine Jackie growing up in this desolate setting. Jackie, with her gleaming blonde hair, captivating smile, and trim figure in secondhand clothes.

Glancing at her watch, she hopped back into the car. It was after eleven. She needed to get to her dad's house and see if there were any messages.

Her father was not at home, but she found the key still tucked in a flowerpot on the porch.

"Really, Dad, this has always been so obvious," she mumbled, inserting the key in the lock and opening the door. She had a feeling her father wouldn't change hiding places, just as he had failed to change so many other things about their home.

The house was empty, still. A sharp pain clutched at her heart as she stood in the dim hallway, listening to the patter of rain on the roof. How quiet, how lonely. It must be awful for her father. She had not been very understanding with him; certainly, she had not shown enough compassion for him when her mother was ill.

Walking back to her room, she parked her overnighter on her bed and dropped her purse on a chair. Placing her car keys on the dresser, she decided to do what she had secretly wanted to do, needed to do, but wouldn't face up to it.

Resolutely, she walked into the bedroom and stared at the

neatly made bed where her mother had wilted away to her death. Her father had refused to put his beloved wife in a nursing home even though relatives insisted she was beyond his care. He had never given up.

She found herself standing at the bed, touching the pillow where her mother's head had rested the last time Tracy was home.

The eyes she recalled were blank; the face was thin and haggard; the hand that Tracy gripped was cold, indifferent. Her mother hadn't known Tracy was home; she hadn't cared.

"But you did care, Mom. I know you did."

Suddenly, all the emotions she had kept dammed up broke loose and poured through her now, sending a river of tears down her cheeks. Her knees buckled beneath her, her stomach wrenched in physical pain.

Laying her head against the side of the bed, she wept brokenly, wishing she could go back and redo the past year, wishing she had come home, even though her mother hadn't seemed to recognize her. Maybe somehow Mom had felt her presence. Maybe some last shred of reality clung to her brain, enough to know that her baby had come home.

She asked for you, her father had said.

She had wanted to challenge him on that, to ask how. Why. Her mother had not spoken in weeks. Why and how could she suddenly find enough strength and presence of mind to call her daughter's name?

The tears continued to flow as she leaned against the bed, her outstretched hand caressing the soft comforter, reaching for the smooth pillow.

She hadn't heard him come in or walk down the hall, but suddenly her father was kneeling beside her, his arm around her shoulders.

"It's okay, honey. Your mom watches over us still."

Tracy lifted a tearstained face to her father, seeing the moisture on his cheeks through the blur in her eyes. "Then does she know how sorry I am, Dad?" she asked, her voice ragged, her throat aching.

"She knows, honey. We all do."

He put his arms around her, and for the first time in years, Tracy sobbed into her father's shoulder and felt the reassuring comfort that her father had always offered.

Twenty

ৎৈ

J ay arrived on her doorstep shortly before five in the afternoon. He looked haggard and tired, and the short-sleeved cotton shirt was soaked to his back in places. The air was muggy and hot after the rain.

"Well, want to take a ride with me?" he asked, a hint of amusement in his eyes.

"You're actually going to let me tag along?"

"You're the one who came up with Woodfin Construction Company. Might as well go with me. I called his office. He told his secretary he was going home early to do some work. We'll see if he's there."

Tracy's adrenaline was soaring as she ran back to freshen up and grab her purse. Jay, who had been so closemouthed, so private about everything, had dared let her in on this. She wondered what his boss would think if he knew a reporter was tagging along on an investigation.

Well, no one else had turned up anything important. Why couldn't she play amateur detective? Hadn't she come up with the suggestion of putting a trace on the pay phone at the club? Maybe she was on a roll.

∽

They drove out to Tommy Woodfin's farm and found him seated on his upper deck. A newspaper lay scattered across the umbrella table.

After getting them a cup of coffee, he invited them to join him out on the deck.

"What brings you two out here?" he asked, slapping Jay on the shoulder.

"Tommy, something came up when we were checking phone records in the DeRidder case. Thought maybe you could help us out," Jay replied smoothly.

Tracy watched Tommy's face, trying to read his thoughts. The expression remained cool, impassive, although his gray eyes narrowed. "What is it?"

"We know Jackie left Green Hills Country Club around twelve-thirty," Jay explained. "At that time, a telephone call was made to your company number from a pay phone at the club. Know anything about it?"

Tommy's eyes narrowed even more, and for a moment, he said nothing. Then, he leaned back in his chair, heaved a sigh, and nodded. "I didn't want to say anything because my company doesn't need any bad press. Neither do I. And it was just a phone call."

Tracy slipped to the edge of the deck chair, anxious to hear what he had to say.

"Jackie phoned me from the club. She had been drinking. Told me she was leaving DeRidder." He hesitated, looking from Tracy to Jay, and back to Tracy. "I'd seen her a few times over the years, and there was still something between us." He put his hands behind his head and stared out at the lake. "You guys remember how we were in high school? Well, I never got over her. She said she felt the same about me."

Slowly his eyes returned to Tracy, then Jay.

"She wanted me to come to Atlanta that day, but I told her no. She was a married woman, that this thing had to stop." His eyes looked troubled as he stared at Jay. "She was upset when she hung up. I don't know where she went or what she did after that. She did say something rather suspicious, though." His eyes drifted to Tracy. "She said there was another man in her life now anyway. That she didn't need me. That he was someone who could help her get some dirt on DeRidder and she could come out of the divorce smelling like a rose."

"Another man?" Jay echoed, frowning. "Who do you think he was? Did she give any indication?"

Tommy shrugged, taking a sip of coffee. "She gave me the impression he was an attorney, or someone in law enforcement who could help her get something on DeRidder."

Jay stared at him. "That's interesting."

"Too bad she didn't drop a name, but I thought maybe she was just trying to make me jealous. She was good at that." He sighed heavily. "That poor DeRidder has been taken for a ride." Then Tommy took a deep breath and looked back at Jay. "That's all I can tell you."

Jay stood, extending his hand. "Thanks for your honesty, Tommy."

"Sure, man. What do you think happened to her? Think maybe she just took off? Or did someone…do something?"

Tracy grimaced at those words. Do something. Like murder. She was confused by what he had told them. Still, if another man were involved, that could explain a lot of things.

Tommy followed them back to the door. "You guys come back out sometime. We'll throw another barbecue. Tracy, how long will you be around?"

"Not long." She smiled at the tall, muscular guy who, in

many ways, had changed little since his days of being a football star. "I'll be heading back to L.A. in a week or so."

"Well, good to see you again." He smiled down into her eyes, a smile that was utterly charming. For a moment, Tracy could see why Jackie had never stopped caring for him.

So what do you think?" Tracy asked as they drove back down the country road in the growing darkness.

Jay was silent for a moment, staring at the road as it wound back up to the gate. "I'm not sure."

"What about this other man who could dig up something on Mr. DeRidder? Jackie must have been getting desperate." She sighed, feeling disillusioned. "I'm disappointed in her, Jay."

"Well, to be honest, the last time I saw her she had changed a lot."

Tracy glanced at him, surprised. She didn't know he'd kept any contact with Jackie. "When did you last see her?"

"Several months ago. It was at a charity function sponsored by United Way. Mr. DeRidder was very active in that."

He fell silent as they drove through the open gate. Tracy waited for him to continue. When she glanced across at him, she was puzzled by the expression on his face.

"So did you talk with her? And what did she have to say?"

"It was just small talk, mainly about my job and a trip she and DeRidder had taken to Europe."

"I don't suppose," Tracy said wryly, "that she mentioned her little hometown."

He shook his head. "No. You know it was almost as if she had blanked it out of her mind, like she never lived there, or if she did it was in another lifetime."

"Well, in a way I suppose it was another lifetime. So how do we go about finding out who the mystery man was?"

Jay was thoughtful again. "Question more people, requestion some who knew her. Somebody is obviously keeping quiet, and that's strange. I wouldn't have expected a lot of loyalty from the people who knew her. What she had with most of them was a very superficial relationship."

"How's that?"

"They seemed to be friendly to her because she was Martin DeRidder's wife. She spent much of her time alone, actually."

She sat in silence, thinking. Jay seemed to know quite a bit about Jackie.

He turned into a small drive-in restaurant. "How about a cheeseburger and a chocolate malt? That's not much dinner, but—"

"But it's exactly what appeals to me," Tracy admitted.

As a waiter appeared at the window and Jay gave him the order, Tracy began to laugh.

"Now what?" Jay looked amused.

"Cheeseburgers at a drive-in restaurant. So Moonglow."

"I'm a Moonglow kind of guy," Jay said, grinning.

As soon as their food was delivered, Tracy removed the wrapper from the straw and dipped it into the thick shake. She gave a sigh of pure bliss. "Now this is living!"

Then her thoughts returned to Jackie. She just couldn't seem to stop thinking about the bizarre story of Jackie DeRidder.

"Jay—" she turned in the seat—"what about the woman she had lunch with at the club—Marilee Champion? Did you talk with her?"

"One of the detectives did. Mrs. Champion claimed they were hardly friends, that they were serving on a committee together and met briefly to set a date for a coffee for committee members. Actually, Jackie didn't have many real friends."

Tracy bit into her fat cheeseburger, not caring about the

179

onions. She frowned, shaking her head. "I'm still suspicious of Mr. DeRidder."

"You've convinced me that maybe DeRidder is worth a closer watch. We've honed in on him, but so far we've come up with nothing."

"From what she told Tommy, I think it's possible he's your lead suspect. Like it or not."

"You may be right."

They finished their sandwiches in silence, then Jay paid the bill and they drove off. Both were deep in thought and didn't bother with conversation until Jay pulled into the parking area before the lake that ringed Moonglow. A full moon sifted silver down through the night, adding a mystic glow to the setting.

"This is still the most romantic spot in the world," Tracy sighed, as the soft summer wind slipped over the oaks and rippled the black velvet lake.

"Yeah, it's nice here," Jay said, looking from the lake back to Tracy's face profiled in the moonlight.

"You know," she laughed softly, "it's kind of funny to be parked here like teenagers, holding hands, looking out at the lake. I don't remember ever feeling so peaceful here."

"Peaceful," Jay said, shaking his head. "My life has been far from peaceful lately—a bombing, a kidnapping, working long, difficult hours to catch criminals. I don't know how I'd make it if I didn't know something about God's peace, even in the midst of chaos."

"Wait a minute," Tracy grinned. "I'm the preacher's kid, remember? I'm the one who should be saying those things. If anyone had a background of faith in the midst of chaos, I surely did. Jay, it's good to hear you say those words," she said, smiling into his face. He had helped her so much, really started her on the road to getting her faith back again.

His eyes drifted over her face. "Well, all I know is that in the midst of all this confusion, you've come along and brought an incredible change to my life. If you're leaving soon, I think I'd better put up my defenses."

"Come on," Tracy teased. "A cool, calm detective like you keeps up his defenses."

"Once, maybe. But not anymore." The expression in his eyes was totally serious.

She decided it was time for her to be honest, as well. "I like you too, Jay. A lot. Too much. Maybe I'm the one who should leave before it's too late."

He reached out, gently pulling her against his chest. "It's already too late."

His head dipped to kiss her lips, and Tracy knew she had never felt like this before. Never.

His kiss deepened, and Tracy pulled back from him. "Hey," she said shakily, "speaking of backing off...."

"Yeah," he sighed, checking his watch. "Wish I could stay in Moonglow so we could take a drive up to the mountains tomorrow. Maybe go to eat at The Dillard House. But I have to return to Atlanta tonight."

"Tonight?" Tracy couldn't hide her disappointment. "You're kidding. That's a long drive back after an exhausting day. I'm sorry you have to leave."

A weary grin touched his lips. "I'm afraid it's part of the job, and a part I don't always like. What are your plans?"

Tracy stared out at the lake. Her plans? Suddenly, her mind went blank. She couldn't believe she was falling in love with Jay, but that was exactly what was happening. So, how was she going to deal with it? Her mind ran over her options and came up with the most pressing thing in her life at the moment: her job.

"I'm going to hang around here tomorrow, and after that I don't know. I'm thinking of asking Sam for another week here, but I doubt that he'll agree to it. I've gotten nowhere on this story."

"Tell him we're about to crack the case," he said, brushing his lips over her forehead.

"Are you?"

"We'll crack it one of these days. I'm just pushing the clock up to give you an edge with your boss."

She laughed. "Thanks. I wish I could believe it was that simple."

"Well—" he turned in the seat and started the engine—"so do I. And as much as I hate to say it, I'd better get going."

Her dad was just getting home from a meeting when Jay drove up. Waving to them, Richard trudged on inside, his Bible under his arm.

"He's a good man, isn't he?" Jay said, staring after him.

"Very good. Things are better between us. We kind of had a heart-to-heart, and I feel a lot better about Mom," she said, studying her hands folded in her lap. "I think I'm making peace with myself...and with God. You know, Jay, I had my first real cry about Mom, and afterwards I began to pray again. It was the first time in a long time. I even got out my Bible and looked up some verses." She looked at Jay. "I guess there are some things I'll never understand. But, as Dad always says, we just have to trust God and go on."

He nodded. "That's right. I need to think about that more than I do in this line of work. It would be easy to get calloused, indifferent. Sometimes I almost do." His eyes drifted over her head to the porch light blazing, then he gave her a quick kiss on the lips.

"See you soon," he said.

Tracy walked up the porch steps, thinking about their conversation at the lake. What good would these feelings do either of them if she left for L.A. next week? She doubted that Sam would extend her deadline; he was pretty hard-nosed when it came to hours and time away from the desk. Maybe, as Jay had said, she could hint that the case was about to crack.

Entering the house, she crossed the hall and saw through the open door to his office that her father was taking down phone messages from the machine.

"One for you," he said, scribbling on a pad.

Curious, Tracy hurried to his desk and looked at what he had written.

Wally. Will call back tonight.

"Wally?" Her father looked a bit dubious. "He was pretty abrupt and impolite. He doesn't sound like someone I'd want my daughter going out with."

"Don't worry, Dad," she laughed. "He's Jackie DeRidder's cousin. And he's already married."

"Do I know him?" her father frowned.

"I doubt it. They live up at the cove in Jackie's old farmhouse, and the woman speaks with a slight accent. I think some of Jackie's relatives moved up north. Apparently, this is a relative who married and brought his wife back to Moonglow. He must have rented the place from Jackie. I forgot to ask about that." She frowned.

So Wally had decided to call her. Excitement filled her—maybe he knew something important. She kicked off her shoes and joined her father in the den, her feet propped up on the ottoman. The TV was turned off for a change as her father flipped through a small notebook. She knew it was the one he kept filled with prayer requests.

"How is your flock?" she asked.

"Two in the hospital, a third expecting a baby any day."

The ringing of the phone interrupted them, and Tracy hopped up. "I'll take it in your office so I'll have a pen and pad."

She hurried into the office, closing the door behind her. If this was Wally, she didn't care for her father's overhearing the conversation. It wouldn't be the first time she resorted to paying for information.

"This is Tracy," she answered. It was a habit long established from working as a reporter.

"This is Wally. Wife said you come up askin' questions today." In the background Tracy heard a roar of voices and something that sounded like the click of cue sticks and balls. Maybe he was calling from the pool hall.

"Yes, I was at your place today, Wally." She gripped the phone tighter. "Can you tell me anything about Jackie DeRidder? Anything that might help in solving her disappearance?"

"What's in it for me?" he asked gruffly.

She closed her eyes, sickened by the fact that Jackie's own cousin must be bribed to help locate her.

"A little money, maybe. Depending on what you tell me. And it has to be something really helpful. Otherwise, I'm not interested."

"I might have something. I talked to Jackie two months ago. She come up to the place to collect the rent. One month it goes to her brother in Detroit, the next month to her. This was her month. I usually mail a check, but she showed up early. I drive a truck for a living, and it so happened I was home that day. I don't know her very well, never been around her much, but she was all down in the dumps. Sat down on the porch and just stared out at the yard. Said she'd made a big mistake."

Tracy listened, mentally assessing whether or not to believe him. "Well, it's pretty common knowledge that she wasn't happy, that she was running around on her husband," she said, testing what he knew.

"That may be what was wrong with her. Said she liked her

lifestyle, didn't want to give it up, but that there was a man in her life, one she was willing to leave DeRidder for."

"Did she say who?"

"Nope. Just said he was going to help her."

Tracy bit her lip. What was it Tommy had told them earlier? An attorney or a man in law enforcement, someone who could help her "dig up" something on DeRidder.

"It's possible I seen her on I-85 that Friday. I was hauling a load of freight into Atlanta when I seen a black Mercedes with a blonde woman driving. It was back this side of Atlanta toward the Lake Lanier turnoff. I'm not sure it was her, so that's why I didn't mention it to the police when they came asking about her."

Tracy's back stiffened. Now, this *was* new information. "Do you know about what time you saw her?" she pressed.

"I left here just before noon. By the time I got that close to Atlanta, must have been around one-thirty. I had a heavy load, so I wasn't driving fast." He hesitated. "I tell you, it sure looked like her. Met her right before you get to the Lake Lanier turnoff. She was by herself."

Tracy bit her lip. If Jackie was headed north out of Atlanta, that might narrow the search. But the fact that she was alone shot the theory that someone abducted her.

"Okay, I have a hundred dollars for you. Does that sound fair?"

"Fair enough. You can take the money up to the house and leave it with Becky. The baby needs some things."

She nodded. "Okay. Thanks, Wally. And if you think of anything else, I'll be here another day or two. Then my dad knows where he can reach me."

She hung up and stared absently at her father's papers stacked neatly on the desk. There was no question now that there had been someone in Jackie's life, someone who could "help" her.

Thoughtfully, she reached into her dad's bookcase and took down a Georgia map. Jackie could have been headed to Lake Lanier, Gainesville, plenty of places. If she was on an errand, she could still get back in time to meet her husband.

But she had been drinking, Tracy remembered. She was not thinking clearly. Maybe she had misjudged her time.

Getting up from the desk, Tracy began to pace the floor, her hand on the back of her neck, her thoughts muddled. This "other man" continued to haunt her. Why had the police and FBI been unable to get a lead on someone else? They knew about the tennis pro. Why couldn't they find out about this "other man"?

Her eyes returned to the phone. She was tempted to leave a message on Jay's answering machine, but she knew he hadn't had time to get home. And what would she tell him, anyway? She was probably throwing a hundred bucks out the window, and yet her instincts told her to stay with Wally, that he was telling the truth. And that he just might think of something else.

She said good night to her father and turned in early. It had been a long, exhausting day, in more ways than one. Her sleep that night was troubled. She kept seeing Jackie, barreling up the interstate in her Mercedes, with Wally chasing after her in a semi. It was a relief when finally her alarm went off and the smell of fresh coffee drifted to her bedroom.

Twenty-one

❧

Tracy made the drive back up to the cove first thing the next morning, five twenties tucked in her billfold. She had refrained from calling Jay because in the daylight of reality, she realized Wally had told her very little. In fact, she felt like a fool paying him for useless information, but she always tried to keep her word.

The old house was as depressing as ever this morning. The difference was, Wally's wife was more friendly to her. She met Tracy at the door, a little grin working at her mouth.

"Wanna come inside?" she asked, attempting to be friendly.

"Thanks, but I'm in a rush." She pulled the money from her purse. "Please, if you hear anything else—"

"Well, there might be."

Tracy hesitated, wondering if this woman could possibly know anything.

"That day she was up here to get the rent, she was pretty depressed. Told me that's what love did to a woman. She had a bandage on her hand, said she stabbed her hand with a treble hook while bass fishing at Lake Lanier."

"Fishing? Lake Lanier?" Tracy repeated. Something in her

subconscious was sending up a red flag. "Your husband thought he saw Jackie in the vicinity of Lake Lanier on the day she went missing. Did she happen to mention who she'd been fishing with?"

She shrugged. "Nope, she wasn't in a talkative mood. Just came after the money and left. Like she said, I guess love can make you pretty sad."

Tracy looked at Becky, seeing a thin, haggard woman with deep lines already forming around her eyes. Had her love for Wally brought the downward tilt to her mouth, or had she always known hard times?

"Are you from around here?" Tracy asked quietly.

"Nah. I'm from Detroit. Met Wally up there. He wanted to come back to the South, but I don't like it here."

"Maybe one day you'll get to go back." Tracy smiled.

Becky nodded and looked wistful. "Wally's getting some money soon; maybe then we can go back."

Tracy had been preparing to leave when those words brought her up short. "Is he getting a promotion?" she asked.

The woman's eyes shifted. "Sort of. I gotta see about the baby. Thanks." She indicated the money Tracy had given her, then stepped inside and closed the door. Standing on the steps, Tracy heard the key turn in the lock.

So Wally was coming into some money. How? And what, if anything, did this have to do with Jackie?

Becky's remarks rumbled around in her head, taunting her...particularly the part about Lake Lanier. Then suddenly she knew why, and her foot hit the brake too hard on a curve. She gripped the wheel tighter as the car swerved; then she gently eased the vehicle left to right and back. When finally she had regained control, she heaved a sigh of relief. She had almost wrecked over...a terrible thought.

Jay had been at Lake Lanier fishing the day of the opening

ceremonies for the Olympics. Surely that was a mere coincidence, wasn't it? But he'd admitted he had seen Jackie recently. And Tommy had hinted at someone in law enforcement... could it possibly be Jay?

"No!" she said, slamming her fist against the steering wheel. "Tracy, what is *wrong* with you? You aren't thinking straight."

If Tommy knew more than he had told them in the beginning, maybe he was still holding something back.

Before she was quite sure what she would say or do, she turned her car in the direction of Woodfin Construction Company in nearby Clayton. She wasn't sure what she was going to ask Tommy, but she had to see him again, try and find out everything he knew.

Jay was at Lake Lanier that day.... He was there, and so was Jackie....

The words continued their ominous chant through her brain. She couldn't shut out their implications, no matter how hard she tried. She drove faster.

The construction company was located a few miles out of Clayton on the road to Moonglow. She parked in the spaces designated for office only, cut the engine, and hurried inside. It was a small office with a receptionist, bookkeeper, and secretary, who led her to Tommy's office, located at the end of a short corridor. He happened to be in.

"Hi, Tommy," she said, after he stood and motioned her into the chair before his desk.

"Tracy, this is a pleasant surprise."

"Got a minute?" Her eyes dropped to the map spread over his desk.

"Sure. Want some coffee?"

She shook her head. "No, thanks."

After the secretary had gone out and closed the door, Tracy came right to the point. "Tommy, have you thought of anything else Jackie told you during that last phone call? Or at any other time? I think the investigators had better start looking for that 'other man' you mentioned."

Tommy shoved his hands in the pocket of his jeans and took a seat behind his desk. "She never specified any names," he said slowly, "and with a city the size of Atlanta, who knows?"

"But you said she hinted he was someone in a position to help her, maybe an attorney?"

"Maybe. Or someone in law enforcement." She could see the idea of another man bothered him, because a deep frown had settled between his brows. "Could have been someone who could prove an embarrassment to the establishment. Know what I mean?"

She shook her head. "Not really."

He stared at her for a moment, saying nothing more. "Tracy, I can't think of anything else to tell you."

She held his eyes for a few seconds. He couldn't or wouldn't. She wondered if the possibility of that other man being Jay had entered his mind as well and he was keeping those suspicions to himself.

"Well—" she came to her feet—"it was worth a try."

"If I think of anything, I'll call you."

"Thanks. See you later, Tommy."

She left feeling that she had accomplished nothing. Tommy hadn't added to her suspicions about Jay. But he hadn't relieved them, either.

At dinner that evening, Tracy's father tilted his head to the side and regarded her curiously.

"You haven't spoken half a dozen words tonight, Tracy. Is something bothering you?"

She speared her fork through her pork chop. "This whole case is starting to bother me."

"Want to talk about it?"

"Frankly...no. There's nothing to talk about. That's the problem. Well, really there *are* a few things...."

She began to tell him what Becky had said to her, moved on to her discussion with Tommy, and finally hinted vaguely at her worries about Jay. She couldn't bring herself to say his name, however. She just referred to someone in law enforcement.

"And you're wondering if Jay could possibly be involved," he said slowly, studying her face as he voiced her greatest fear.

"Oh, Dad, I would never suspect Jay of...anything," she replied quickly, but she knew her words lacked conviction.

"Tracy, I think I'm a pretty good judge of character. Jay is an honest and honorable man. No matter how things may look, I just don't think he is capable of doing anything criminal."

Her eyes searched his face, eager for the reassurance he offered. "I'm so glad to hear you say that. It's not that I suspected him, it's just that...."

"I understand. But let me hasten to add that I have been wrong about someone a couple of times in my career as minister. Only God can read the heart."

She nodded, thinking he was always so wise, so right.

"I appreciate your honesty. Think I'll go do some work now. I have a couple of pages written on Jackie's background. I need to go over them."

Tracy had brought along her notebook computer, and she typed for the next hour. This time the words came easier. Jackie was still an enigma to her, but the background story was coming together now.

She heard the phone ringing but assumed it was for her father. Then he knocked gently on her door.

"Come on in," she called.

He handed her the cellular phone. "Jay would like to speak with you."

Tracy took the phone and hesitated, still confused by her emotions. Her father closed the door softly. She took a deep breath before she answered.

"Hi, Tracy. What's going on?" Jay asked.

"I'm trying to get some work done," she answered, hoping she didn't sound as cross to him as she did in her own ears.

"Oh. Sorry I interrupted you then. I just called to say hello, see if you turned up anything else."

She bit her lip, feeling the sting of tears in her eyes.

"Not really," she answered, sick at heart. How could she suspect someone like Jay? Her dad was right. He was an honorable man; he would never do...whatever had been done. "Have you?"

"Unfortunately, no. We're questioning DeRidder a bit more thoroughly, but his alibi sticks. And the thirty minutes he was out of the office has now been backed up by the newspaper man on the corner, where he bought a newspaper, turned, and went back inside his building."

"Hmmm. So do you think he couldn't have met someone around the newspaper stand?"

"Newspaper man says he didn't."

She sighed. People had been known to lie for enough money.

"To be perfectly honest," he continued, "we're getting nowhere. It's a circus down here, anyway. I've been stuck chasing down leads on another murder. And the town is still tense after the bombing. I'm ready to retreat to the woods and become a hermit."

She smiled sadly. "You don't mean that. You thrive on your work."

"Just as you do."

She nodded, thinking that this was another reason that she had to forget him. They were both workaholics in jobs that would never bring them together again. Although one never knew in this business. Another CNN reporter had moved to L.A., but she knew that Jay would never do that.

"Know when you'll be back in Atlanta?" he was asking.

She sighed. "Probably in a day or two."

"Will you give me a call?"

"Sure. And thanks for calling, Jay."

By the time she hung up the phone, she felt absolutely wretched. Jay couldn't possibly be the "bad guy" in the Jackie DeRidder case, and she felt sick for even suspecting him. What was wrong with her? She was getting desperate, that was what. She had to call Sam first thing in the morning and beg for more time.

Jay sat staring at the phone for a full minute. What was wrong with Tracy? There was a distinct difference in her voice. He frowned and thought about her, despite the ringing telephones and his monstrous workload. It occurred to him that he had depended on her company quite a bit to distract him from the stress of his job lately. What was he going to do when she returned to L.A.?

He got up and wandered over to the coffee machine, his frustration mounting. There had never been a girl like Tracy in his life. He was falling in love with her, and he knew it. What could he do about the situation? Should he be honest with her about his feelings?

A deep sigh wrenched his body as he filled a Styrofoam cup with black coffee that looked two days old. She was going back to L.A., and there was nothing he could do about it. What if he told her how he felt? Would it make a difference? He stared into the coffee, oblivious to the fact that he was being paged.

Tracy's troubled thoughts didn't go away once her head hit the pillow. She tossed and turned and dreamt of being dressed like a policewoman chasing Martin DeRidder through the streets of Atlanta.

At two in the morning, she reached for the clock and peered miserably at the numbers. Groaning, she put it back down, punched her pillow, and sank down again.

Good morning, God. I'm talking to you more these days. But please open the door to this mystery. Find Jackie. Tell someone where she is. Please. And forgive me for doubting Jay. And bless him.

She took a long, deep breath, feeling better after her prayer. At last she drifted off to sleep, but her sleep seemed more like a nap than five hours. When the alarm went off at seven, she put the pillow over her face and groaned, hoping the alarm button would magically shut down on its own. It didn't. Finally, she rolled over, shut it off, and forced herself out of bed. Her body felt as though she had been in step aerobics for the first time in six months—and the instructor had been a real taskmaster.

After a hot shower, a shampoo, and a generous serving of the oatmeal her father had left on the stove for her, Tracy felt more prepared to tackle the day.

In assessing her moves, an idea came to her. Since Tommy was the last person who spoke to Jackie, or the last person they knew of, maybe Jackie had mentioned a name. Just to taunt him. She recalled Jackie was the type of person who enjoyed making guys jealous. If Tommy had turned her down, why wouldn't she say something to taunt him? Perhaps she *had* and

Tommy was trying to protect someone. She didn't want to think about who that *someone* was. In a way, she knew this was a wild-goose chase, but it was her last goose to chase.

She dressed in jeans and T-shirt and hurried to her car. As she drove through the streets of Moonglow, she waved to a friendly face here and there. She had to admit that it was good to be home, but as soon as she made her morning phone call to Sam, she felt certain she would be making her plane reservations.

When she arrived at the construction company, she was told by the receptionist that Mr. Woodfin had gone into Atlanta today. Thanking the young woman, she was headed back to the parking lot, glancing absently toward the rear of the building. There she spotted Wally. She did recognize him from their high school days, after all.

She froze.

He was crossing a concrete parking area where half a dozen trucks were parked.

"Wally!" she yelled to him. "Could you wait a second? I'm Tracy Kosell, and I need to talk with you for just a minute."

He whirled, and as he saw her approaching, she caught a flash of guilt crossing his face. Or at least she interpreted the look as guilt. Why?

"I'm in a hurry," he said. "Got to make a run to Dillard."

"Then I won't keep you. Do you work here?"

His eyes dropped momentarily as he fumbled with the insignia on his T-shirt, which identified him as an employee of Woodfin Construction. She had worked at her job long enough to know when someone was hiding something or was caught lying.

"Yeah, I work here. But I gotta get going. And I haven't thought of anything else to tell you."

Did I ask? she thought sarcastically.

"I just wanted to say hello," she said, stepping out of his path.

A sullen look crossed his face as he nodded and strode off toward his truck. She turned and walked back to her car, her mind spinning. What was wrong with him? Why did he look like a bully who had just kicked a little kid?

Because he had done something wrong, or something suspicious. She was certain of it. When she reached her car and got in, she sat behind the wheel, staring at the big truck as it roared out of the back parking lot.

So he worked for Tommy. She hadn't thought to ask the name of his employer when she spoke with his wife. She recalled his wife had mentioned that Wally was coming into some money. Was that money from Tommy's pocket? Maybe Wally was nowhere near Lake Lanier that day, maybe he never saw Jackie, as he claimed. Maybe he was told to mention Lake Lanier to throw anyone off the track.

Jay had mentioned fishing at Lake Lanier in his conversation with Tommy when they first went to the cookout. In fact, the only reason she had become suspicious of Jay was because Tommy had mentioned "someone in law enforcement." Then Wally had dropped Lake Lanier in his conversation.

That was it! Tommy was deliberately trying to throw them off the track.

One of the waitresses at Smoky's Barbecue had been off the day she questioned them about seeing Jackie. But Smoky had a sharp eye. What if the black Mercedes had been Jackie's car, after all? Smoky's place was only a half mile before the turnoff to Tommy's farm. When Tommy wouldn't come to Atlanta, maybe Jackie had, on impulse, come up here.

Another idea came to her now, and she started the car and drove home to pick up something. Ten minutes later, she was pulling into the parking lot at Smoky's restaurant.

Twenty-two

❧

Smoky was not at the barbecue pit, to Tracy's disappointment, but upon entering she saw a tall, athletic-looking waitress, lightly sunburned, filling orders behind the counter.

"Are you the one who's been on a backpack trip into the mountains?" Tracy asked casually, settling onto a stool at the counter.

"That's me. I'm Jan."

"Hi, Jan," she replied, extending her hand. "I'm Tracy Kosell. My dad is a regular here."

"Reverend Kosell! Sure. He's a sweet man. How much barbecue does he need?" A broad smile zipped over her round, sunburned face as she reached for a pad and pen.

"One plate for each of us. Oh, and a couple of orders of your blackberry cobbler."

"Good choice." The girl grinned, writing down the order.

Tracy lingered at the counter, waiting for Jan to hand the slip through the window to the cook.

"Jan, on that last Friday you were working, before you went on vacation, do you remember waiting on a blonde woman, late twenties, about five feet five, well dressed?"

Jan chewed her lip thoughtfully. "Smoky asked me that, and I'm not sure if I have my days straight, but there was a striking blonde woman in here either Thursday or Friday. Got something to go. I didn't see what kind of car she left in; Smoky asked me that too." She leaned closer, lowering her voice. "He showed me that newspaper picture, but I can't be sure it was the same woman. She was wearing sunglasses that day she was here, and, well, she just didn't talk like I figured Mrs. DeRidder would talk."

"Wait a second." Tracy hurried back out to her car and reached for the high school yearbook she had gone home to retrieve from the back of her bookshelf. The picture of Jackie in the newspaper made her hair appear darker, and the expression on her face was not quite right.

Taking the yearbook back inside, she flipped to the pages that showed Jackie as class beauty, then as head majorette.

"Now look at this picture—and remember it's about nine years old—but you see the way she smiles? And I understand her hairstyle had changed since the newspaper picture was made. She was wearing it shorter, like here...." She found a picture that resembled the way Jay had described her looking now.

Jan stared at the pictures, then looked at Tracy. "Funny thing, this looks more like the woman than those pictures I've seen on TV and in the newspaper. The woman I remember didn't seem as old as the one they've been showing on TV."

"Could it be because she was in a frivolous mood?" Tracy asked quickly. "Maybe like she had been drinking?"

"Yeah," Jan said, nodding her head. "If you wanna know the truth, she was real giggly. She sure didn't act like a society kind of woman. Not that I would know," she added with a laugh.

Tracy's heart was pounding faster; she was onto something

and she knew it. "Do you remember what she ordered?"

She shook her head. "No, I get too many orders to remember one in particular. Unless I drop it," she added, laughing. She looked back at the pictures in the yearbook, chewing her lip again. "I do remember her order was for more than one person. Don't know how many. I think it was a pretty big order. Maybe a whole slab of ribs."

Tommy is a big eater, Tracy thought. She could feel her "gut feeling" take over, the one she relied on when a story really got rolling and she knew she was heading in the right direction.

"Do you remember what she was wearing, Jan?"

Jan took a deep breath, her eyes drifting over Tracy's head to the ceiling, as though trying to picture her again. "No, just something nice. I remember worrying about spilling barbecue sauce on her. But she came and went in a flash, like she was in a real big hurry. Wait a minute!" She pressed a hand to the side of her head, as though trying to concentrate. "There was something about that order. I remember worrying she would spill it." She stared at the tile floor for a minute. "I know." She snapped her finger. "She asked for an extra order of barbecue sauce. 'Tommy likes a lot of sauce,' she said."

Tracy stared at her, mesmerized by those words for several seconds. She fought an impulse to throw her arms around Jan and give her a big hug.

"You've been *very* helpful, Jan. Thank you so much."

Tracy was mentally putting the pieces of the puzzle together with lightning speed, and she liked the fit. Her hunch was right; she knew it. Jackie had driven up to see Tommy that day.

"Oh, your order is up." Jan said, turning to sack up the barbecue and cobbler.

Tracy dived into her purse, pulling out her wallet. Pushing a few dollars into Jan's hand as a tip, she gave her a big smile.

"Look, I appreciate your help."

"No problem." She gave Tracy another wide grin. "Good luck."

Tracy quickly paid the bill and hurried home. She would surprise her dad with lunch…and Jay was about to get a call from the first pay phone she could find.

Jay was going on his last nerve today. He'd spent a sleepless night, and the fact that nothing else had turned up in the DeRidder case was not helping his day go smoother. The department was getting a lot of pressure from the media, as well as the public, to solve the case. Not to mention the higher-ups. The mayor had phoned his boss just this morning.

He poured himself a cup of the strong coffee, flinching as he did so. He should be drinking something to soothe his nerves, not make them worst. At that moment, one of the guys poked his head from an office cubicle and yelled to him, indicating the telephone.

He forgot the coffee and bolted to the phone.

"Hi, Jay. It's Tracy. Look, I may be onto something. Would it be possible for you to come back to Moonglow today?"

He hesitated, wondering what was up. "What's going on, Tracy? This sounds important."

"It is important. I may be chasing wild ducks, but see what you think about this theory."

He listened intently as she ran through her story, beginning with the information from Wally's wife about his coming into some money. She covered her visit to Tommy's office, being straightforward about his innuendo about *law enforcement*, and then Wally's reference to Lake Lanier.

Jay gripped the phone tighter, glancing at his watch as she paused to draw a breath. She explained the fact that Wally worked for Woodfin Construction, then capped off the entire thing by the waitress who had almost positively identified Jackie as being in Smoky's that day and had even mentioned the name Tommy.

"This could all be spitting in the wind, Jay. But—"

"But I'm coming," he said matter-of-factly. "I'll be at your house in a couple of hours."

"Thanks, Jay."

He smiled into the phone. "You're the one who should be thanked."

He hung up, gathered up his pager, notebook, and pen, then bolted out of his office. Maybe at last they were onto something.

Twenty-three

꙳

"Thanks for lunch," Tracy's father greeted her, as soon as she breezed through the front door.

"What?" She stared at him. "Oh, sure." She dashed to the bathroom to freshen up.

"Aren't you going to join me?" he called after her.

"In a minute."

After redoing her hair and freshening her makeup, she entered the kitchen where her father was happily spooning into his cobbler. "Decided not to wait on you."

"Good idea."

"What's up?" He studied her thoughtfully. "You look like you're back on top of things again."

"I am. And Dad, I'm glad for this opportunity to talk with you. Let me run a theory by you."

She took a seat at the kitchen table, making a grab for her barbecue sandwich. It felt good to be sitting here chatting with her father, like high school days when she would get his opinion on a school project. As always, he was a careful listener, trying to see all sides to the theory.

"You may have something, hon," he said, chewing thoughtfully, staring into space. "I'm glad you called Jay. You don't need to be pursuing this any further on your own."

She nodded, bolting her sandwich down. Let him think Jay was bringing a SWAT team with him. She didn't want her dad worrying about her; he had enough to cause him concern just keeping up with his flock.

An hour later, Jay was knocking at her door, which meant he had made the trip to her house in less than an hour and a half.

"Hi," she smiled, opening the door. "Had lunch?"

"I grabbed a hamburger on the run."

"We really must do something about your eating habits." She grinned at him.

"About your theory," he reminded her. "Let's get right on it."

"I'll grab my purse."

As soon as they were in Jay's car, headed toward Tommy's farm, she ran over her information again. "Don't you think it fits, Jay?"

"Better than anything else we've been able to put together." He frowned. "I have a theory of my own. It's such a shot in the dark, I hesitate to mention it."

She leaned closer, tapping his arm. "I'm a sucker for a shot in the dark."

"Well, the land that adjoins Tommy's is where the trout lakes are being built."

Tracy stared at him. "And so...?"

"We could hear the bulldozer equipment going the day we were at the cookout, remember?"

Tracy nodded, chewing her lip. "You aren't thinking...."

"It's too wild to put into words, but I just want to see what the Glover farm looks like. Since it's Saturday, I don't think anyone will be working on the construction site. Let's have a look."

"Sounds like a good idea."

The smoke was spiraling high and heavy as they passed Smoky's place on the Hiawassee Road. In the front seat, Jay had stacked some maps, and now he pointed at them. "Would you dig out the topo map for me?"

"Sure." Tracy began to flip through them. There was a forest service map and a highway map.

"Here it is," she said, lifting one up from the bottom of the stack and spreading it out on the dash.

The map showed a large scale of the localized area, with the contour lines of the ridges and valleys and streams.

"What's your plan?" she asked curiously, looking from the map to Jay. He was passing the turnoff to Tommy's farm, and continuing on down the highway.

"We're going to do a little snooping on our own, check out the area where we heard the machinery going that day. And I think I remember Tommy saying his company was doing the work there."

"So?" Tracy frowned.

Jay was leaned back in the seat, one arm casually steering the wheel. "So I've known of cases in the past where a new dam site was a burying ground. In other words, it's easy to hide a body that way."

"Oh," Tracy said, staring wide-eyed at the contour map. She hadn't gotten that far with her thinking. She'd always known it was possible Jackie had been murdered, but she'd preferred to just think she was missing. "Oh, man. That's a pretty gruesome thought, Jay."

"Then where is she? And where's the car?"

They had continued on up the highway approximately a mile and a half and were dropping off a ridge into a valley. Just ahead was the bridge that stretched over South Fork Branch.

"Let me see that topo map," Jay said, pulling to the side of the road.

Tracy handed him the map. He studied it momentarily, then picked up the highway map and studied it briefly. "We turn here," he said, indicating a narrow road that veered to the right just before crossing the bridge. He laid the map aside and glanced back at the topo map on the dash.

"Now put your finger here," he said, indicating the spot, "and help me follow the route back to the farm."

With her finger she traced the road that followed the valley near the branch all the way to the point where Rabun Creek and South Fork Branch came together.

"The road continues on into the valley to a white spot," she informed Jay.

"That's a farm or an open area that would have been a farm at one time."

"The rest of the map is green."

"That's forest," Jay informed her.

"I'm getting a good lesson in topo maps," she said, glancing back at the road.

"I'm thinking the white area is probably the Glover farm."

He pointed to the spot where her finger rested. "See, a little further west down the creek is another open area that should be Tommy's farm. The two farms are separated by a long finger of woods."

Tracy put a hand on the dash to brace herself as the road became rough and unmaintained. They followed along on the south side of the branch, which, in places, was six to eight feet wide, working its way east and southeast.

Then the valley widened with large beautiful trees.

"This is the national forest," Jay said. "That's why the trees haven't been cut. This is probably an old forest-service road that has been kept open."

Masterfully, Jay threaded his way between a mud hole and the trunk of a giant beech tree with half a dozen sets of initials carved into the smooth, white bark.

Rounding a bend, the road opened up into a parklike area with giant trees and knee-high, lush grass.

"South Fork Branch empties into Rabun Creek about here," he said, pulling off the road to a wide place that appeared to have been used for a parking area over the years. "Let's get out and walk."

"This is a gorgeous place," Tracy said, opening the door and breathing in the clear air and listening to the creek roaring its way out of the high country.

They began to walk the path along a valley, looking up to a high bluff of rock outcroppings. They could see where campfires had been built over the years, with burned ends of ashen logs and rocks still piled up. The road opened out into a narrow meadow, where cottonwoods and willows formed a line along the creek bank.

"There're the lake sites." Jay pointed.

Tracy could see where a small lake was being built and was already filling with water. Another hundred yards or so down the creek was another lake.

"That second one has just recently been completed," Jay said. "You can see how the lakes are built on the west side of the creek so the water can be diverted out of the creek to fill the lakes."

They walked briskly along the road that passed to the right of the lakes.

"Someone is here." Jay pointed to a pickup truck parked on the side of the hill. Heavy equipment was parked near the site where the dam was being built. A man stood beside the truck, but he had begun to walk in the opposite direction.

"Apparently, he hasn't heard us over the roar of the creek." Just as Jay spoke these words, the man turned and stared, then waved to them.

He was a tall, robust man, sixtyish, with white hair and a pleasant face.

They picked up their pace, hurrying to reach the man's side as he waited for them.

"I'm Jay Calloway." He extended his hand. "Would you happen to be Mr. Glover?"

With a smile the man returned his handshake. "Yes, I'm John Glover. I own this place."

"Good to meet you, Mr. Glover. This is my friend, Tracy Kosell. We're originally from Moonglow, but at the present time, Tracy lives in California, and I'm in Atlanta."

"I see. Well, my wife and I moved to Clayton about three years ago. I'm retired from a construction company in Dothan, Alabama. My wife and I fell in love with this part of north Georgia about ten years ago when we visited her brother, who lives in Clayton. I heard about this piece of property being for sale, and we decided to put in some trout lakes since we both like to fish. Maybe someday we'll build a cabin over there." He indicated the parklike area.

"It's beautiful," Tracy said, looking around.

"I understand Tommy Woodfin's company is putting the lakes in for you," Jay continued smoothly.

John Glover nodded. "That's right. Originally, I had planned to do the lakes myself, but due to some health problems a couple of years ago, I decided to hire the work done." He grinned. "I can't stay away, of course. Every now and then when a piece of equipment is idle, I climb on and do a little work because I enjoy it. Tommy doesn't mind; I reckon it helps him out a little."

"We know Tommy," Jay said. "He lives on the other side of those woods, doesn't he?"

"That's right. In fact, he often walks through the woods to check on the progress of the lake, see how his men have done."

Jay nodded, turning to survey the site. "So how's the work going?"

The man frowned for the first time. "We should have been finished a couple of weeks ago, but we've had a little problem here at the spillway." He pointed to the spillway built in the edge of the hill.

"Oh, what's the problem?" Jay asked, crossing his arms over his chest.

Watching him, Tracy was amazed at how adept he was at getting information from people through what seemed an innocent conversation. He really was a great investigator, and she respected his talent now more than ever before.

Mr. Glover had paused before replying, scratching his head as though puzzled. "You see how the dam juts up against the side of the hill. We cut out a place for the spillway, but we've had two rains in two weeks that washed out the side of the dam where the spillway was. Because the ground was wet, it's taken longer to get in and repair the spillway. We repaired it once, and then it blew out again. Now we're having to pack it down good and refill it."

"I know the spillway has to work properly so as not to break the dam," Jay said, nodding thoughtfully. "Did your other spillway hold up okay?"

"As a matter of fact, it did. Due to the heavy rain, the other lake is filling up faster than I expected. We're going to do a little bit of smoothing around the outer edges, cut it around the high water mark so the weeds won't grow so badly around the edges."

"Mr. Glover, I was just wondering about this particular dam. Being in the construction business, do you understand why you've had problems with this spillway?"

Mr. Glover shook his head. "No, as a matter of fact I don't. The original dirt coming off the hillside was solid. It shouldn't

209

have washed the way it did just because of the rainwater. Normally, if there's a soft spot or an area that will erode, it would be the other side of the dam near the creek, where field dirt was hauled in."

Tracy turned to Jay, and suddenly she realized how his questions were gently leading the man toward a bigger question. She, too, was wondering if it were possible that something was under that dirt, causing the problem when it rained.

"Do you remember the day the spillway first washed out?" Jay asked.

"Oh...two weeks ago, maybe longer." Then he looked at Jay, and his eyes brightened. "You know, I just remembered it was early in the morning on Saturday when we had the heavy thunderstorm in a short period of time. My wife and I were relieved the rain was localized, that it wouldn't rain out the first day of the Olympics. Later in the day I drove out to check on things. That was when I noticed the spillway had washed out, leaving a two- or three-foot ditch. It was right this side of where the bulldozer and front-end loader were parked."

"Mind if we take a look?"

"Nope. In fact, I was just about to get on the front-end loader and do some work."

Tracy and Jay followed John Glover over to the end of the dam to where the equipment was parked.

"You see, we had to haul in ten loads of field dirt just to fill in around here so we could pack it down. I was just thinking of spreading some of that dirt out when I saw you two."

He glanced back at Jay and frowned. "You sure do look familiar. Are you in the construction business?"

"No, I'm a state investigator, Mr. Glover. I'm up here working on a case."

Recognition flashed in Glover's eyes. "You're the detective I've seen on television. You're working on the DeRidder kidnapping in Atlanta, aren't you?"

"Yes, I am."

"Mr. Glover," Tracy spoke up, "I'm a reporter from the Associated Press. I've been assigned to cover this story simply because I'm from the area. You see, Jay and I went to school with Jackie and Tommy Woodfin."

Glover's eyebrows hiked as though he was slowly beginning to make the connection.

"Jackie and Tommy were sweethearts in high school," Tracy said, then bit her lip, wondering if she'd said too much.

"Mr. Glover," Jay explained, "we have some evidence that points to the fact that Jackie may have been in Moonglow on the afternoon of her disappearance, possibly even in this area. You seem puzzled over the fact that the side of the undisturbed hillside washed out after the heavy rain two weeks ago. Would it be possible for it to wash out if, say, a hole was dug there and not properly filled back in?"

John Glover stared for a moment, then automatically his eyes darted toward the woods separating his farm from Tommy's.

"That could explain what's wrong with this levee if the ground wasn't compacted back as hard as it had been originally." He started toward his front-end loader. "As I told you, I was really over here to dig some of that loose dirt, so if you guys will get back on the edge of the hill," he pointed, "we'll see what's causing the ditch to wash out."

Jay was staring intently at the spillway. "That's a good idea, Mr. Glover."

They watched as Glover walked over and got on the front-end loader and started it up. Black smoke boiled out from the pipe as he pulled down and started digging large bucket loads of dirt, placing it on the low side of the dam.

"This may be my wildest theory yet," Jay said under his breath.

"I don't think so," Tracy answered solemnly.

Glover kept working until he had an eight-foot-wide trench from the back side of the dam all the way to the front side next to the hill.

"How deep is that?" Tracy asked Jay.

"Five, probably six feet," he answered, his arms crossed over his chest, as he continued to stare at the ditch.

Suddenly there was a grinding sound, of metal striking metal. Almost instantly Glover backed up the front-end loader, dropped the bucket down to the ground, and cut the engine.

Tracy and Jay rushed up and crawled down into the ditch to look at exposed black metal.

Jay looked at Tracy. "Bingo."

"Well, young man, you were right," Glover said, staring in amazement. "There's something buried there. And I'd guess it to be a black car."

"I'm going to my car to use my cellular phone," Jay replied. "We can't touch anything else until I call my office in Atlanta, requesting a search warrant. And I'll contact the Rabun County Sheriff's Department."

Tracy wondered how Jay could move so quickly when she stood rooted to the spot, her eyes frozen on the black car fender.

"Oh, Jackie," she whispered, shaking her head. "Why did it have to end like this?"

Twenty-four

Jay and Tracy were back in the car, speeding toward Tommy's farm.

"What are you going to do?" Tracy asked, still bewildered by all that had happened.

"I'm going to give him a chance to confess before I read him his rights."

Tracy closed her eyes, still feeling sick. "Maybe Tommy didn't really do it. Maybe it was someone else."

"And maybe that isn't Jackie's car," Jay sighed. "I'd like to think that we're wrong, but I'm afraid not."

Jay turned onto the road leading out to Tommy's ranch. Tracy was thinking about the Friday afternoon they had driven out this road to the cookout, feeling relaxed and totally unprepared for what they would discover only a week later.

"The gate's open," Jay said, steering the car along the road that veered left and gradually wound its way down hill. "That means he's probably home."

The road dropped over the last low hill, and Tracy stared sadly at the house nestled cozily beside the lake. She couldn't help thinking about Jackie driving down this road for the last time.

"Oh, Jay—" she turned in her seat, shaking her head—"I pray that we're wrong."

Jay glanced at her with a worried expression in his eyes. "We'll soon find out."

He pulled into the driveway behind Tommy's construction truck and cut the engine. Before they were out of the car, Tommy appeared at the door, a beer can in his hand.

He did not smile as they approached him; he merely looked from one to the other, his eyes solemn.

"You two look like you just lost your best friend," he finally spoke.

"Maybe we did," Jay said gravely as they climbed the porch steps.

"Come on inside," Tommy said, looking into Jay's eyes as though trying to read what he was thinking. "What are you guys doing up here, anyway?" he asked, his tone rather abrupt. All pretense of friendliness was gone now.

"Tommy, I'm afraid this is an official visit," Jay said. "We're pretty sure we've found Jackie's car buried under Mr. Glover's dam. An official team is on the way to bring it up. If it happens to be Jackie's car, you're in big trouble, pal." He hesitated, watching Tommy carefully. "If you confess, it could go easier for you."

Tommy turned weary eyes to Jay. There was no life left in their depths, only misery. He looked as though he had died a dozen deaths already.

"I guess there's no need to ask why you suspect me?"

"A witness placed Jackie at Smoky's that afternoon. She was buying barbecue, and she mentioned your name," Jay said. "And once we go over the car, and *if* she's there, I expect your fingerprints and hair fibers will show up. Then it's murder one, buddy."

Tommy slumped into the nearest chair. "What difference does it make if you go easy or not? I've already killed myself. I'm just a walking corpse now."

Tears filled his eyes and began to trickle down his tan cheeks. He dropped his head, attempting to conceal some of the pain that ravaged his face.

"It was always there...the love, the pain." The words sounded as though they were torn from his throat. "I couldn't be happy with Lisa for thinking of Jackie. And all DeRidder's money didn't satisfy Jackie. Last year, she called me...said she wanted to see me. We started meeting...it's gone on for almost a year. I asked her to leave DeRidder, come home and marry me. But she didn't want to give up the money. She said she'd been poor all of her life and she liked what he could give her. But she wasn't happy, and she would never have been happy with the social life, with that lifestyle. It wasn't her, you know?"

He placed his beer can on a table and lifted a work-roughened hand to swipe at his cheeks.

"I told her I wasn't rich but I had a good business here...that we could be happy together. She promised to think about it. Then the next time we were together she said maybe she could get a good settlement from the divorce. She was going to talk to DeRidder. That was the week before the Olympics."

He hesitated, closing his eyes. Tracy could only stare at him, horrified by his words.

"She called that Friday from the club, wanted me to come down there, but I refused. She said she was going to leave him, had figured out a way. She wanted me to meet her at the farm."

Tension stretched between them like a tightrope. For several seconds, nobody spoke or moved. Then Tommy continued speaking in a monotone.

"I left work, got here about the time she did. We were about to have lunch out on the deck. She had been drinking...I could see she was in an unreasonable mood. She said she wanted me to figure out a way to knock him off." He covered his face with his hand. "I thought I was above murder. Told her I wouldn't stoop to killing the man. She said it was the only way, that he wouldn't agree to a divorce."

He pulled himself weakly from the chair and walked toward the sliding glass door and opened it. "Come out here," he said.

Tracy glanced at Jay, who was watching Tommy carefully. They slowly approached the deck that crossed the upper side of the house along the rear. About sixteen feet below, the concrete patio extended from the game room, where he had hosted the party, to the edge of the yard.

Tommy walked slowly toward the wooden railing that encased the upper deck. His shoulders slumped as he planted his hands firmly against the rail and glanced around. He looked as though he had aged ten years in the last half hour. "We were sitting here," he said, pointing to a patio table nearby.

Tracy stared, trying to see in her mind's eye Jackie, drinking, demanding that Tommy get rid of her husband. She closed her eyes; it was too horrible to conceive.

"I refused to go along with any plans, told her she was drunk, that she would feel different when she sobered up. Then she went into a rage," he said, fresh tears filling his eyes. "Told me I didn't love her, wouldn't help her, all of that. She got up and slapped me; I stood up to defend myself. She picked up a beer bottle and aimed it toward my head; I knocked her back. When I did she fell against the railing here...."

He pointed to a small wooden strip of railing. It was not aged like the other wood; in fact, it looked as though it had just been installed in the past week.

"The nail was loose in this piece of wood. She went back with a force that broke the wood...."

He covered his eyes with his hand, as though he could no

longer look at the terrible scene. "Fell down to the concrete," he said, his voice muffled by the fingers that covered his face. "I ran downstairs." He was sobbing now. "When I reached her, she was lying on the concrete, her body twisted…her neck broken. There was no heartbeat.… I knew she was dead."

Jay and Tracy stared at one another, completely horrified. To think this happened to their old schoolmates, two people they had known all of their lives.

"I covered her up and sat down, wondering what to do." Tommy sank into the patio chair, cradling his head between his hands, his elbows propped on his knees. "I knew I should have called the police, but I kept thinking about DeRidder and his money, how his lawyer could make me into the other man who murdered her in an act of rage. I knew how much money it would take to fight him in court…my company's already in debt."

He paused, lifting his wet face to look from Jay to Tracy with bleak, wet eyes. "It seemed kinder to just bury her up here at Moonglow. She always wanted to come home; I knew she did. So when it got dark, I wrapped her up and put her in the trunk of her car, then drove the car over the back road to the lake sites. There's nobody within miles of here after construction shuts down. I got on the front-end loader and hot-wired it to start it. It was easy. I dug up a hole at the dam site, pushed the car down in it, then got back on the machine and covered up the hole. She was at peace, safe. The press couldn't make her out to be a drunk or an adulteress; she just went missing. I read all the time about people who disappear. Thought it was best for her sake to have it appear that she was kidnapped and never found."

In the background they could hear the sharp cry of a siren approaching Tommy's property.

"Tommy, they're coming."

He shook his head. "It doesn't matter. I'm as dead as Jackie. I don't care about anything anymore."

Staring into his face, Tracy could see this was true. All emotion had been drained through his tears, his confession. He was only a shell of a man. She turned away, sick at heart.

Jay began to read him his rights just as a black-and-white car, along with an unmarked white car, roared to a halt in the driveway. She started to walk back down the steps, her knees trembling, her words coming with great effort.

"He's already confessed," she said as half a dozen men swarmed onto the front porch.

She walked past the men, heading back toward Jay's car. She couldn't bear to watch anymore, hear anything else. She was expected to be a cool-minded reporter able to do her job. As she sank into the front seat of Jay's car and buried her face in her hands, she hoped she never became so "cool" that she was immune to human suffering. She began to weep, her heart overflowing with despair for two wasted, misdirected lives.

When Jay returned to the car, he could see from the tears rolling down Tracy's face that she was extremely upset. He closed the door gently and reached forward to cover her hand with his. "I know it's hard to understand. I deal with lots of situations that are heartbreaking. If it weren't for my faith that God is ultimately in control, I could become calloused and bitter like some detectives I've seen."

Tracy sniffed, squeezing his hand. "I don't see how you do it, Jay. No, let me retract that statement. It's your faith in God and your attempts to see his ways in every situation. You've been so good for me," she said, wiping her eyes, then glancing back at the house. "As sad as this entire situation has been, it's helped me put my own life in perspective. I think of Tommy and Jackie...." She choked as fresh tears spilled down her cheeks. "It could have been so simple. They could have been just another couple who fell in love in high school, got married, and lived their lives together here, at this farm. Had children, been happy."

"It wasn't that way though, Tracy. Don't forget, we human beings have wills of our own. We make our own choices, sometimes right, sometimes wrong. To Jackie, money was the choice."

"The god," Tracy said dully. "It was the driving force in her life, the thing that caused her to compromise her values, forget who she really was. It drove her beyond reason, beyond conscience. It was her idol," she said, shaking her head. "Right now, Jay, I'm getting my priorities in order. I've let my work be my driving force for years; I wanted to be the best."

"There's nothing wrong with wanting to do your best."

"There's something wrong when it clouds your judgment of all else. I've become materialistic. I see that. Just think; Jackie put material needs above everything. It clouded her judgment, and she turned into someone she was never meant to be." She took a deep breath. "I'll be in Dad's service tomorrow morning."

"May I join you?" he asked, brushing his lips over her forehead.

"I would be very pleased to have you join me. And maybe I'll even try to prepare a lunch for us afterwards. We can pretend to be just another typical Moonglow couple."

"Sounds good to me," he said, starting the engine and backing out of the drive.

Tracy did not look back; she did not want to see them loading Tommy into the police car. And she was grateful that Jay did not have to return to the lakes. She had no desire to see the car...or the body in the trunk.

Twenty-five

The church bells pealed merrily across Moonglow on Sunday morning. Tracy stretched lazily in bed, trying to absorb all that had happened in the last twenty-four hours: discovering the horrible truth about Jackie…and Tommy. But it was over now, and her life must go on.

She took a deep breath, rubbing the sleep from her eyes. This was going to be a good day, she decided. Jay was coming over to attend church services with her. Beth, Ken, and the children had invited them for Sunday dinner afterward. Her dad was ecstatic, and to her surprise, so was she. *Guess I'll have to find another time to impress Jay with my culinary ventures,* she thought wryly.

She threw back the covers and headed for the shower.

Richard Kosell's church resembled one on a Norman Rockwell Christmas card—a slim steeple topped a white frame church situated on a grassy knoll. The parking lot was filled today as regular churchgoers greeted one another and climbed the steps to the double front doors. The interior was cheerful, with red carpet, white pews, and stained-glass windows.

Tracy chose the same seat as always, third row, piano side. It was a standing family joke; only today Jay was seated beside her, and this was not a joke. She was filled with a sense of joy—and relief. She knew how she felt about Jay, and she had the impression his feelings were the same. They were in love. Only God could bridge the gap of career and distance, and she knew that. But God was still in the miracle business, her dad often reminded her.

Beth and Ken came through a door at the back of the sanctuary, herding their children to second row, piano side. Jay stood and shook hands with Ken, then gave Beth a hug. The children stared up at him with huge, curious eyes before being marshaled into their seats and shushed as the music began.

The choir, wearing red robes with white satin collars, entered from a side door and filed dutifully to their chairs, lifting the songbooks and waiting for the song director to signal their opening.

Soon the organ and piano had reached a crescendo of "How Great Thou Art" and leveled back down to accompany the choir as their voices rang out sweetly on this Sunday morning.

Tracy felt her chest swell with pride as her father entered the pulpit and took his seat, casting a warm glance in their direction.

He walked to the podium and smiled out at his rapt audience.

"This morning I will be reading from the Book of Psalms, chapter 143, verses 5 through 8."

As Richard Kosell opened his Bible, Tracy's eyes slipped to Jay, wondering what he thought of her father. Jay was wearing a navy suit with white shirt and a conservative tie, and her heart beat faster as his hand slipped over to find hers. They held hands and smiled at one another, not really caring who saw.

She turned her attention back to her father, already reading the Word.

"'Let the morning bring me word of your unfailing love, for I have put my trust in you. Show me the way I should go, for to you I lift up my soul.'"

Show me the way I should go.... The words seemed to hang in Tracy's brain. *What a good prayer*, she thought. *Maybe if I referred to Psalms more often, I wouldn't feel like a feather blown in the wind, spinning in all directions. Maybe I could be grounded once again.*

As her father closed the Bible and began to speak, Tracy was captivated by his words, realizing again what wisdom he imparted, how close he lived to God, and how devoted he was to his congregation. To anyone who needed him.

"We are all students of life," he was saying, "and every day is an education. When times of testing come, as they always do, we hold tight to God's truth, for he is with us. With that knowledge, we can face heartache and grief and the daily challenges of life. As students of life, we should see each challenge as a learning experience, and with this learning experience, let us move a step closer to God. God is in charge in our lives; we need to allow him to do what's best for us."

Tracy swallowed, fighting back the sudden rush of emotion that filled her. As she sat in the pew on this beautiful morning, feeling the solid comfort of people around her who had cared about her for years, an odd peace settled in her soul. Why had she allowed her future to be such a puzzle? Why couldn't she see God's plan before now? For suddenly it came to her clearly and distinctly.

She would come home. Maybe she had always wanted to come back, but her ambition had driven her on and on, wanting more and more. She thought of Jackie and shuddered. Closing her eyes momentarily, she breathed a silent prayer.

God, never again let me be blinded by what I think the world has to offer. Never again let me forget what you have always taught me: The only real satisfaction in life comes from peace in the soul. And with you I have that peace again.

Later, after a huge Sunday meal of roast beef with all the trimmings at Beth's house, Tracy and Jay wandered out to the backyard and settled into a couple of yard chairs beneath a giant oak. Beth was putting on a video for the children in their room, and Ken and Richard were in the den, discussing an item to be rehashed at the next deacon's meeting.

"It's been a good day," Jay said, watching with amusement as Tracy kicked off her high heels and moaned with relief.

"A great day," she said, smiling across at Jay.

"Here, do this," he said, reaching down to lift her ankles and place her feet across his lap. "Better?"

"Better." She grinned. "I hate wearing heels."

His fingers moved over her stockinged feet, gently massaging. The stiff muscles began to relax beneath his kneading fingers.

"Good grief, you could make a fortune doing this."

"The idea of massaging just any woman's feet doesn't appeal to me. You're special."

Tracy tilted her head and looked at him. "How special?" she asked softly.

He continued to knead her feet as his eyes fastened on hers. "I'm in love with you."

She gasped, almost yanking her feet away.

"Does that surprise you?"

She stared at him as tears welled suddenly in her eyes. "No, it pleases me. More than I can say. Because the same thing has happened to me."

"You two want a cup of coffee?" Ken yelled from the back door.

Jay and Tracy jumped involuntarily, then whirled to stare blankly at Ken.

He grinned. "Am I interrupting something?"

"We'd love a cup of coffee," Jay called back. He turned to Tracy. "So what are we going to do? Commute from Atlanta to L.A.?"

She shook her head. "No. I'm coming home, Jay. I think I could be quite content working in Atlanta again. And I shouldn't have any trouble getting a job back at CNN. As a matter of fact, I think I might prefer to do that for a while."

Jay leaned forward, cupping her chin in his hand. His mouth moved over the soft contours of her lips as his kiss became more urgent.

"Wait a minute," Tracy pulled back breathlessly. "Do you realize we are sitting in Beth's backyard, probably putting on a show for the neighbors? And I think I see Dad's face framed in the kitchen window!" she said, staring at the house.

"Then I may get thrown off the property," he said, dropping her feet and glancing back toward the house.

"I don't think so. Why don't we go inside and be sociable? I think Dad needs to know that his sermon was especially good today. I certainly found my direction again. And yes, Jay, I do want to come home."

They were standing, holding hands, gazing into each other's eyes. "Then we can work everything else out," he said, squeezing her hand.

Hooking her high heels over her fingers, walking barefooted, she fell into step with Jay. As they started walking back to the house, the verse her father had spoken echoed once again in her mind.

Show me the way I should go, for to you I lift up my soul.

225

She had asked for guidance and found it, and now she wanted to shout her happiness from the rooftops.

"Thanks," she murmured, glancing up at the sky.

"Me, too," Jay said, as they climbed the back steps and opened the door to the smells of home and happiness.

Dear Reader,

The Olympics were a monumental period of history for 1996. I wanted to do a story that would touch on some of the events, while covering parts of the great city of Atlanta. As always, my fondness for the mountains and the people of North Georgia crept into the story and thus the little community of Moonglow was born.

Most Georgians will recognize Moonglow as a part of Rabun County, and it was a pleasure meeting some of the people in this area and hearing of their history.

So many people in today's world have conflicts with job situations or locations when it comes to relationships. I wanted to write a story to exemplify that God can show us the way to work out these problems if we ask...and wait for his answer. I also wanted to use characters who looked in the wrong places for answers, like Jackie DeRidder. Forgive me, if that part of the ending seemed a bit tragic. However, we see it and read it every day, and I do hope my stories reflect the real world in which we live. That's why walking in faith is so important.

I'm very excited about my new romantic suspense series using Jay's older brother Michael and his wonderful wife, Elizabeth. I hope you will follow the series with the first book, *Promises*.

Bless you for reading my books, and my prayers are always with you.

Love,

Peggy Darty

Write to Peggy Darty
c/o Palisades
P.O. Box 1720
Sisters, Oregon 97759

If you enjoyed reading *Moonglow*, the following is an excerpt from Peggy Darty's next novel, *Promises*, the first title in a new romantic suspense series that follows the lives of Michael (Jay's older brother), his wife, Elizabeth, and their young daughter, Katie.

In *Promises*, Elizabeth, a Christian psychologist, has a client with serious problems caused by her elusive twin sister. Elizabeth enlists the help of Michael in finding this dangerous sister before it is too late. In the process, a new romance blooms between Michael and Elizabeth as they discover the joy of falling in love again.

Prologue

January 1976

It is a cold winter day in rural north Georgia. The Chattahoochee River, sluggish with ice, winds past a lonely looking shack built on stilts for protection against the river's overflow. Johnni Hankins huddles beneath the shack. She is eight years old, with even features beneath a mop of red hair. She is dressed in ragged jeans and a torn sweatshirt. Her head is tilted back, listening to the angry voice of a man inside the shack.

Suddenly the door flies open. Julie, a twin to Johnni, dashes onto the porch. She is a frail child with short brown hair. She, too, wears ragged jeans and a sweatshirt. She runs down the steps and heads toward the woods.

Tom Hankins explodes onto the porch. Fortyish, he is a large man with unkempt red hair and red beard, wearing overalls and scuffed boots.

"Julie, you'd better tell me where she is!" His gruff voice grates into the silence of the gray day.

Julie runs fast, arms pumping, feet flying. As she casts a glance over her shoulder, her face is a study in terror. She has promised to take care of Johnni, her mischievous twin. *She has promised.* If her father finds Johnni, there will be another beating. If only there were someone to help them…but there is no one. Bessie, her neighbor, speaks of a God, but she has only heard the word coming out of her father's mouth in vile curses.

"There you are!" She can hear his voice bellowing in the background. She stops running and whirls in panic. He has found Johnni. She has broken her promise again.

One

September 25, 1996

Oak Shadows Plantation sat on five hundred acres of towering oaks and stately pines. The plantation stretched to the river, once the shipping point for the cotton kingdom that had ruled Oak Shadows. But that was long ago. The cotton fields had not been farmed in years, and the grounds were in need of tending. Nevertheless, in the center of the plantation, the house held dominion like a brave yet aging mistress. It was a house that still took one's breath away, despite its need of paint.

Four thick, white columns rose past verandas on the first and second stories to a tiny cupola perched on the third floor. The lower veranda still held the promise of hospitality, with old oak rockers and an ancient swing.

Inside the house, the front parlor that had once been the sewing room for Confederate garments was now an office, furnished with a pleasant blend of old and new. Prized antique pieces were well placed among contemporary items, such as the traditional desk, where Elizabeth Calloway sat, looking across at Julie Waterford.

"This is quite a coincidence," Julie was saying. She spoke in a soft, shy voice. "I had no idea my new neighbor would be my psychologist, but this arrangement suits me perfectly. I developed agoraphobia a few months ago. I can no longer be in crowds. That's why I stay out of Atlanta."

"Atlanta can be pretty intimidating," Elizabeth Calloway said with a gentle smile. Elizabeth was a tall, slim blonde with classic features, warm brown eyes, and a gentle smile that her clients found reassuring.

"I was raised here at Oak Shadows," Elizabeth went on. "This place goes back four generations. My great-great-grandfather was a Confederate soldier. There is even a wild rumor that my great-grandmother was a Confederate spy. Both are buried in the family cemetery, and some of the locals like to say that Jenny—that's the Confederate spy," she laughed, "strolls the grounds when the moon is full."

"What do you think?" Julie asked, wide-eyed.

"I don't believe in ghosts," she answered quickly, "so the tale never bothers me." She hesitated, glancing up at an antique chandelier. "My parents were living in Atlanta when I was born, but when my dad was killed in Vietnam, Mom and I moved back to Oak Shadows. I stayed until I went away to college. When Grandmother died last fall, I inherited this place, and I've always loved it. So Katie and I came home."

She watched Julie's eyes drop to the simple gold wedding band on Elizabeth's left hand. Elizabeth sighed. "My husband stayed in Atlanta." She said nothing more. How could she explain the complicated separation that had torn their little family apart?

"I didn't mean to pry," Julie said in a rush. She was a small woman with short brown hair and pale brown eyes behind gold, wire-framed glasses.

"You weren't prying," Elizabeth responded gently, then looked down at the open file on her desk, reading the notes she had taken on Julie. Julie's husband, Dr. Malcomb Waterford, had been killed in a car accident over the Christmas holidays. "I'm sorry about your husband," she said, looking back at Julie.

"He was a highly respected psychiatrist."

"Thank you." Julie lowered her eyes again. "It's been a rough year."

"And now you want to find your twin sister?"

"I want to stop her."

Elizabeth's eyes widened, although she had learned to keep her facial expression calm and composed. "Stop her?"

"She's jealous of the way my life has turned out. By that, I mean I had good parents, a good education, and I married a man of status, although Malcomb was fifteen years older than I and quite wealthy. Johnni's life—" She broke off as tears trembled in her eyes. "Johnni and I were eight years old when a social worker came and—" she swallowed hard, turning to stare through the window to the branches of the towering oaks, starting to turn gold in the September light.

"You were placed in foster homes?" Elizabeth suggested, hoping to make the conversation easier for Julie.

Julie's eyes drifted back to Elizabeth. "I was adopted by a wonderful couple, Phillip and Sarah Harris. They've retired to Key West."

"I see."

"A few months after Malcomb died, Johnni called me. She said she had found me. . .and that she still hated me."

"Hated you?" Elizabeth could not conceal her surprise.

"I broke a promise to her. As a result, our lives changed drastically." She began to sob. "I'm not ready to talk about this."

"I understand. Perhaps if you could just see Johnni face-to-face rather than have these phone conversations...."

"She makes terrible threats," Julie sobbed, coming to her feet. "I really must go." She reached for her purse.

Elizabeth pressed her hands against the desk and stood. "I want to help. Let me give you something to take home with you." She placed the Book of Psalms into Julie's hands. "You said you aren't a believer, but if you'll just read a chapter now and then, I think you'll find strength and comfort in the verses."

"Thanks." Julie dabbed at her eyes with a Kleenex. "I'll call for another appointment."

She swept past Elizabeth and hurried out to her sleek gray Mercedes, parked in the circular driveway.

Elizabeth followed her to the door, staring after her. Julie Waterford was a woman on the brink of a nervous breakdown. Of that Elizabeth was certain. This sister, Johnni Hankins, had to be found. And the person who was best at finding people was her husband, Michael Calloway.

She sighed, closing the door. Hugging her arms against her chest, she thought of Michael. Their careers had always been in conflict, and yet she had always known that Michael was the best at his work. His agency was called Searchers, Inc. She and Michael had once joked that he searched for lost people while Elizabeth searched for lost souls. Both were on different missions, and yet, in some ways, their goals meshed.

She glanced down at her gold wristwatch. Soon it would be time to pick up Katie at school; only today was Friday, and Michael was picking her up from school. He avoided Oak Shadows—and Elizabeth herself—as much as possible. Michael was taking Katie to a Braves game this evening.

Tears swelled in her eyes. She should be going with them; how had this terrible thing happened to them?

She wandered back to her desk and glanced down at the picture of rosy-cheeked Katie. Blonde curls framed an oval face with huge blue eyes and a warm smile, guaranteed to melt the coldest heart. Katie was almost eight, the same age Julie had been when she was placed in a foster home. The mother had died, she assumed, or left the girls with their father, who must have been a brute of a man.

Elizabeth's life had not been without trauma, but she had always known she was loved. And she had the capacity to love. She still loved Michael; she still was committed to the promises she had made on their wedding day, even though they were living separately. Those marriage vows had been sacred to her, and Michael claimed to feel the same. Yet, they couldn't seem to work their way through this terrible fog that enveloped them as they drifted further and further apart.

Maybe she would speak with Michael about Johnni Hankins. Someone had to find her...and someone had to stop her from the torment she was causing Julie. She returned to her desk and sat down, thinking about Julie Waterford. Julie reminded her of a dainty little bird who had fallen from its nest and been stepped on by cruel people. Elizabeth so wanted to help her as she had the others who had come to her for counseling. This was the driving force that had sent her back to college for her Ph.D. in psychology.

Staring at Julie's file, Elizabeth thought of a colleague in Atlanta whom she had mentioned to Julie. This was a doctor who could offer her more help than Elizabeth. But when she mentioned this to Julie, she had refused. She wanted to work with Elizabeth, no one else. And she was not yet healed of agoraphobia. She had her groceries delivered; her mail was dropped at her mailbox, and a simple visit to Elizabeth's house seemed to throw her into a state of confusion.

Elizabeth got up from her desk and wandered to her well-stocked bookcase, pulling down a book on agoraphobia.

Michael and Katie burst through the door of his apartment chattering with excitement about the Braves game they had just attended. Katie's cap was missing from her tumbled blonde curls; a mustache of mustard outlined her mouth, with another smear staining her jacket. Michael looked at her and chuckled.

"You gotta hit the tub, sweetie. Your mother would be upset with both of us if she could see you now."

Katie turned dreamy eyes to her father. "Daddy, we had a good time, didn't we?"

"Are you kidding? When Chipper Jones hit the winning home run, I've never heard such an uproar in Fulton Stadium. You know it's the last season of games in that stadium, hon. They're tearing it down to build a new one next year. That's why we gotta win the series!"

Katie turned to stare up at her father. He was tall, dark, and slim. His face was dominated by deep blue eyes, and she thought he was the greatest guy in the world. She just didn't understand why he and Mom didn't live together anymore.

She sighed heavily, tugging off her jacket. "Dad, I wish you still lived with us."

The happy expression that Michael had worn since Glavin struck out the first batter now wilted from his face. A dark frown ridged his forehead as he tilted his head and looked sympathetically at his daughter.

"Hey, you and I still have fun, don't we?"

Katie's blue eyes turned pensive. "Yeah, but…" Her voice trailed off as the blue eyes, so like her father's eyes, drifted into space. She was thoughtful for a moment as Michael searched for the right thing to say.

"Mom keeps that beach picture of us right by her bed," Katie volunteered in her most confidential tone. "And sometimes she cries," she added softly.

Michael heaved a sigh and sank into his recliner. "And sometimes I cry too, Katie."

Katie looked shocked. "Oh, Daddy! You don't cry."

Michael put an arm around his daughter, squeezing her tight.

"There's nothing wrong with a man crying when it hurts, Katie. Have I taught you differently?"

She tilted her head and looked sideways up at her dad, her blue eyes wide and thoughtful. "No."

"Well, we're learning a lot about life together, pal. Now…off to the tub and your pajamas. I have a new book to read to you at bedtime."

"A new book? Great!" With a squeal of delight, she dashed up the stairs.

Michael still lived in the townhouse he had shared with Elizabeth for the past six years. Before that, it had been a one-bedroom apartment, with Katie's bed across the room from theirs. Maybe every woman wanted a big house; was that it? Was that what had pulled Elizabeth out to Oak Shadows, a sprawling old relic filled with history—and ghosts, according to local accounts. Neither he nor Elizabeth believed in ghosts, but he always wondered how Katie would feel if the gruesome subject were mentioned to her.

He heard the bath water running in the tub, and his mind switched back to the words she had spoken earlier.

Dad, I wish you still lived with us. He should have come right out and said it: "Your mother and I are both too stubborn for each other, Katie." But he had kept silent. It seemed childish and downright embarrassing for two adults to be locked in a mental tug-of-war, particularly when Katie was on the loosing end of the rope. But how could he run a thriving detective agency when he lived thirty minutes away, up in the country? He supposed he could hop into the car at two in the morning and head into town when a distress call came in. Or they could spend their weekends at Oak Shadows, as he had suggested to Elizabeth.

The other problem was, he hated the place—absolutely hated it. Or was it really the Turner money he hated? *Come on, Calloway, tell the truth,* his conscience nagged. He was a poor farm boy who had scraped his way up the ladder to being labeled one of Atlanta's most successful businessmen. And he had done it through blood, sweat, and tears. Oak Shadows had been handed to Elizabeth on a silver platter, like so many things. One of them had to give in, grow up. And neither seemed ready.

This was hard, really hard. "God, help us," he said quietly, closing his eyes and leaning his head against the back of the chair.

He was taking Katie to his parents' farm up at Moonglow tomorrow. The grandparents hadn't seen her in weeks. He had tried to keep the news of his separation from Elizabeth a secret from them, but there was no way he could hold it back any longer. And he didn't want to set the wrong example for Katie by misrepresenting the facts, or outright lying. He would simply tell them the truth…but it wasn't going to be easy. He was almost looking forward to work on Monday. He was a workaholic and he knew it, admitted it, but it blotted out some of the pain in his life.

Monday…work… With those thoughts he pulled himself from the chair and dragged himself to the kitchen to rustle up a snack.

On Monday morning, Michael Calloway stepped off the elevator, the newspaper inches from his face, as he walked down the corridor past several offices, pausing at the wooden door with

SEARCHERS black-lettered across the center of the door. Scanning the sports section, he fumbled for the knob, opened the door by remote, and entered his office.

"The coffee is made."

He closed the paper and smiled across at Anita Jackson, a tall woman in her fifties, with graying hair, a few wrinkles, and a pair of kind hazel eyes set in a pleasant face. She had been the model of efficiency, and Michael continually counted her among his blessings. She was organized, intuitive, dependable, and knew exactly how he liked his coffee. Furthermore, she wasn't above delivering a mug to his desk.

"Have I told you lately that I appreciate your hard work?" He looked across at Anita with a kind smile.

She nodded. "But I always like hearing it. You've had half a dozen calls already."

Michael sighed, glancing around his neat office. The reception area was small, with a plaid sofa and matching chairs placed opposite a coffee table stacked with magazines, all arranged by Anita's perfect hand.

He headed for his office, thinking of the day ahead. The room was large, conservatively decorated in greens and browns. A mahogany desk and swivel chair dominated the room, with a Queen Anne chair positioned opposite the desk. The walls held wildlife prints along with an autographed picture of the Atlanta Braves. It was home for him, the only place that was not a tomb of loneliness since Elizabeth and Katie had moved out.

The thought pierced his heart like a spear as he recalled the weekend: the tears his mother had shed upon learning that he and Elizabeth were living apart.

"You two made a promise the day you spoke your wedding vows," she reminded him with a sob.

"I know, and neither of us want a divorce. But just let us

work this out on our own," he had pleaded quietly. With the wisdom typical of his mother, she had dropped the subject and gone in search of her granddaughter, perched on her grandfather's knee, listening to the latest fishing tale.

"Ready to make chocolate chip cookies, Katie?" she had inquired. Later, she had then offered to drive Katie back to Elizabeth on Sunday, sparing Michael the pain.

Michael removed his navy blazer and hung it in the closet beside the door as Anita entered with a steaming mug of coffee.

"You look nice this morning," she observed, looking him over. She persisted in saying that, according to her age, she could be his mother. He doubted that. Still, she looked after him with much the same care. Her eyes swept down his pin-striped, red-and-white shirt, to the navy slacks. Michael knew she was patrolling for loose threads, missing buttons, a dry cleaning tag.

"Glad I pass inspection," he teased, gratefully accepting the coffee. "Did I tell you I'm placing a star on our church tree in your honor?"

"You did, and I'm touched. Now about those calls—"

He put up a hand. "I'll return every one of them. But I gotta tell you, Anita, I'm tired of finding husbands who don't want to be found."

"What about children who *want* to be found? The mayor still brags about your finding his son. You might want to return this call first," she said gently, noting the pink slip.

It was Elizabeth at home. Since he dealt with danger on a daily basis, his first thought was of Katie, but Anita was quick to reassure him.

"Everything is fine. She just wants to talk with you about one of her clients."

"Oh." There was frost on the word as he sipped the coffee, staring at the telephone number.

"Come on, Michael. It's the pot calling the kettle black when you complain of her being too devoted to her work."

"I never said that," he replied, reaching for the phone as Anita hurried out of the office, tactfully closing the door behind her. His hand hesitated on the key pad as he cradled the phone against his cheek and thought of Elizabeth.

When her voice came on the wire, his breath caught in his throat. Just the sound of her voice still brought a rush of emotion to him, but he tried to push aside his feelings and get to the reason for her call.

"Hi. Anita said you wanted me to call you. What's up?"

There was a moment's pause, and he couldn't help wondering if she, too, was assaulted with a mixture of emotions when she heard his voice.

"Katie and I are fine. She had a great time over the weekend. And it was good to see your mother again. I'm calling about one of my clients," she rushed on, the breathless quality of her voice a signal to Michael that she wanted to avoid their personal lives.

"Your client?" he repeated, puzzled. She never discussed her work with him anymore. He fumbled with his coffee cup, curiosity mounting as he waited for her reply.

"I'm dealing with a very troubled woman—my neighbor, actually—who is desperate to find her twin sister. The sister, Johnni Hankins, is apparently psychotic. She calls Julie, making terrible threats. Julie has caller ID, but Johnni always places her calls from pay phones."

Absently, Michael reached for a pad. "You must be concerned for your client if you're calling me about her. What, exactly, do you want me to do?"

There was a momentary pause. "I want you to locate Johnni for us. Julie Waterford lost her husband this past year, and that was tough enough. Now this twin sister, who, by the way, was separated from Julie at the age of eight, is insanely jealous because Julie has money and property and apparently Johnni has had nothing but poverty and problems. I know it doesn't make sense, but I'm afraid if this twin isn't stopped, Julie is going to have a breakdown. She's very close now. You're the best at finding people, even I have to admit that, Michael."

"That's quite a compliment coming from you."

"Could we just leave personal issues out of this? Julie is able to pay well for finding her sister. Why don't you just go see her? Talk to her? She owns the farm adjoining mine...."

The farm adjoining mine. Those words bit at Michael in the worst possible way. Ever since Elizabeth had inherited Oak Shadows, there had been nothing but problems. Now she had the audacity to ask him to go to her neighbor's farm, when he hated the thought of being within a mile of Oak Shadows.

"Elizabeth, I don't make house calls."

"Michael, this woman has agoraphobia. Fear of crowds. She never goes into Atlanta."

He couldn't stop the heavy sigh that escaped his chest.

"Please, Michael." The voice was soft and persuasive and sent a jolt all the way to his socks. He closed his eyes, pressing the receiver tighter against his cheek. He couldn't say no to her, he knew that. But then again, he couldn't just cave in the first time she called. He decided to try to strike a happy medium.

"I'll have my secretary make an appointment with—what is her name?"

"Mrs. Malcomb Waterford. Her husband was a highly respected psychiatrist who taught at Emory."

He nodded. "I've heard of him. I'll see what I can do."

"Thanks, Michael." Her voice softened, but the ache in his heart intensified.

"You're welcome," he answered. "And by the way, you have a neat daughter."

"Maybe she's a bit like her father."

He sat up straighter, pleased by the compliment.

"Gotta go," she said suddenly, as though needing to backtrack, erase the compliment, stifle all hope of reconciliation.

"See—talk to you later," he amended.

Before he could reflect further, Anita was at the door, announcing the arrival of his first appointment for the day.

He was glad. He didn't want to think about Elizabeth.

"Before I talk to my client, see if you can set me up with Mrs. Malcomb Waterford. I'll go out there," he said hastily. "Tell her Elizabeth asked me to come."

Anita smiled warmly. "I'll be glad to do that."

He grinned wryly, knowing she liked Elizabeth.

Michael slowed at the driveway that ran beside a small, wooden sign lettered WATERFORD FARMS. He guided his black Jeep up the winding driveway past landscaped lawns to a red brick mansion, then parked carefully in front of the sprawling structure.

"Hello, Tara," he sighed, looking over the imposing mansion. He could never feel at home in a place like this. He tried not to think of the adjoining farm, Oak Shadows, or the relic of a house which Elizabeth hoped to restore to its former grandeur.

His eyes traced the thick, white columns of the elegant mansion before him. He just didn't fit into places like this, not Michael Calloway, a farm boy from rural Moonglow in north Georgia.

Well, he was here. Might as well go on with the plan.

He got out of his Jeep and climbed the crescent steps, glancing absently at a miniature marble statue on the front porch. He rang the doorbell and waited, thinking about what Elizabeth had told him about Julie Waterford.

The door opened, and a tiny woman with short brown hair and brown eyes peered at him through wire-rimmed glasses. Dressed in a white silk blouse and black slacks, she cradled a white Persian.

"Hi. I'm Michael Calloway." He nodded at her, glancing again at the cat and thinking of a kitten he had once rescued for Katie.

"I'm Julie Waterford. Please come in."

Michael stepped over the threshold into a marble-tiled foyer with a broad circular staircase that seemed to float upward to the second and third floor. His eyes dropped back to the foyer, to the three abstract paintings placed along the wall.

"Those are not my best work," Julie said, following Michael's eyes to the paintings.

"You're an artist?" Michael inquired, looking back at the smudges of color that made no sense to him.

"I try to be an artist. Come into the den."

Michael followed her into a large room with oak paneling, overstuffed sofas and chairs. In the far end of the room, a stone fireplace was flanked by bookshelves loaded with books. A black Persian leapt from the arm of a chair, arching his back at Michael.

"Out of the way, Lucifer," Julie scolded softly, then glanced over her shoulder at Michael. "He's the mischievous one. Angel here is a love." She smiled at the white cat in her arms as she deposited her on the sofa. Lucifer scampered out of the room, leaving Michael with the distinct feeling that he was an unwelcome guest in Lucifer's domain.

Michael's eyes swept the room, lingering on the oil painting of a middle-aged man with a thin face, keen blue eyes, and receding brown hair.

"That's Malcomb." Julie sighed. "He was a brilliant man. Have a seat, Michael."

"Elizabeth tells me you need to find your sister." He decided to come right to the point.

Julie nodded. "Her name is Johnni. She could have been married once, but she still goes by her maiden name. Hankins."

Michael removed a small notepad and pen from his coat pocket. As he wrote down the name, he glanced back at Julie. "Do you happen to have a photograph of your sister?"

"Follow me."

Keeping an eye out for Lucifer, Michael cautiously followed the tiny woman back through the door, across the hall to a large room with cream-colored walls and red accents in the oriental rug, loveseat, and chair. A coffee table held an assortment of pictures. At the far end of the room, an easel was placed beside a table holding small pots of paint and charcoal pencils in a ceramic jar. Beyond the easel, a glass wall overlooked a long meadow leading to a dense woods.

"Nice view," he said, aware for the first time how beautiful the land up here was. He had closed his eyes to the beauty when he came to Oak Shadows with Elizabeth, but now, begrudgingly, he could see why she was pulled back to her roots.

"After we married, Malcomb converted this room into a studio for me," Julie said.

Michael walked over to look through the glass window. A deer had come out of the woods to feed. It was nice to think about Katie seeing wildlife in her backyard, and yet he worried about his family's safety.

247

"Oh, you see the deer out there?" Julie asked, her voice little more than a whisper. "Malcomb planted green fields for deer and hired a biologist to establish a quail habitat."

He nodded. "Good idea."

"You asked about a picture." She had returned to the coffee table and picked up an antique frame holding a photograph.

"Here's Johnni. It's the only picture I have."

Two little girls dressed in playsuits stood in front of a gray shack. One girl had brown hair and dark eyes, the other girl had striking red hair and green eyes.

"I can't tell much about her," Michael said, tilting the photograph for a better look.

"I wish I could do a sketch for you, but I'm only good at abstracts. Our features are similar, but our coloring is different, as you can see. And our personalities. I tend to be shy as a mouse. Johnni has never been afraid of anything except—"

She turned back to the coffee table, replacing the picture.

"Except what?" Michael prompted.

"I'd rather not talk about our father."

"Okay." Michael nodded, pursing his lips. *That's what you pay my wife to listen to,* he thought, wishing he didn't feel so bitter about Elizabeth's work. He tried not to think about what Anita had said, but he knew it was true. They were both devoted to their jobs, and those jobs had eventually wedged their way into the heart of their marriage, killing off all their spare time together.

"Any other sisters or brothers?" he asked, pushing his mind back to Julie's family.

"No. The seventeen-year-old girl who gave birth to us died when we were two years old. I doubt that she ever had proper medical care. We were very poor."

Michael cleared his throat. "I understand you and your sister were separated when you were eight years old."

Julie took a deep, long breath. "I was fortunate enough to be adopted by wonderful people. Things did not go well for Johnni." She placed the photograph on the table and began to pace the room nervously. "I had not heard from her in years. After Malcomb died, the phone rang one day, and it was Johnni. 'I've found you,' she said."

Julie's brown eyes lit up for a moment, and Michael could see that she would be an attractive woman if only there were any light in her face, but the eyes were dull and lifeless until now as she spoke of finding her sister again.

"I was so lonely. Naturally, when Johnni called me, I was thrilled. But as we talked, I began to see what the years had done to her. She had grown very cynical." She ran a hand through her short hair and paced more furiously. "She refused to talk about her personal life, so I didn't press her. But she became angry, quarrelsome. She said some terrible things to me." She closed her eyes for a moment, swaying slightly.

Michael reached out to steady her. "Hey, are you okay?"

She nodded. "I'm okay. I have to be okay."

"Do you think your sister is in Atlanta?" he asked, glancing over his shoulder at the photograph.

"She said she was, but she wouldn't leave an address or phone number. Can you find her?"

"Atlanta is a big city."

"You might start your search at the Peachtree Hotel. She said she was calling from a bar there."

He jotted that down in his notebook. "Tell me more about her."

"We both turned thirty in June. I believe she may be a very beautiful woman. She told me her hair is the same shade of red. Red like maples in the fall. It's her most distinguishing feature.

And her eyes are a vivid green. She has an oval face, like mine, and was fortunate enough not to have freckles, despite the red hair."

A thought occurred to Michael. "Do you have a recent photograph of yourself? I noticed in that one—" he indicated the two little girls—"the two of you were almost identical except for the coloring."

"You want a photograph of me as I look now?" she asked, obviously puzzled.

He nodded. "I'll have an artist change the hair and eyes so I can show the picture and ask around. Does she have any scars or distinguishing features?"

Julie shrugged. "I don't know about scars now; she had none the last time I saw her. How on earth would you find her from a photograph of me?" She couldn't seem to get past that.

"Maybe I'll get lucky." He grinned. "Maybe there's still enough resemblance that someone at the Peachtree Hotel will remember her. Maybe she still goes there. I follow all leads."

She still looked puzzled as they walked back to the den and she picked up a five-by-seven color photograph, handing it to Michael.

Michael studied the picture. The photograph featured a woman who looked quite different from the one he had met today. Her short brown hair was neatly waved, her features were enhanced by a light covering of makeup, and her brown eyes held a pleasant expression. Losing her husband has almost destroyed her, he decided. His eyes scanned the white Georgian blouse she wore in the photograph, then returned to her face.

"That picture was made a year ago, shortly before Malcomb died," she explained.

Michael nodded thoughtfully. "Do you need this back?"

"No, keep it." She cleared her throat as Michael started toward the door.

"Listen," she called after him, "I don't know what kind of people she hangs out with...." The light was gone from her eyes; her features had that pinched expression once again. The change in her was remarkable, Michael decided, realizing why Elizabeth had said she was a woman on the brink of a breakdown. "Be careful."

"Don't worry about me." He smiled reassuringly. "It was a pleasure meeting you."

She appeared to be forcing a smile; her lips looked stiff, tense. "You have a lovely wife," she said, opening the door for him. Her eyes drifted toward the woods in the distance, as though seeing the land beyond.

He sighed. "Yes, she is. I'll be in touch."

He hurried back to his car and got in, cranking the engine, wondering if he should drive on over and see Katie. Glancing at his watch, he realized it was not yet time for her to get out of school. But Elizabeth was probably home. As he reached the end of the driveway, he braked and stared bewildered at the road before him. Should he turn right and drive back into Atlanta? Or should he turn left, drive up to Oak Shadows, and have a talk with Elizabeth?

He sat staring blankly at the road, thinking of Elizabeth and Katie, feeling torn with conflict. He still loved Elizabeth. He always would.